JOHN PAUL II

MY BELOVED PREDECESSOR

JOSEPH RATZINGER
BENEDICT XVI

Edited by Elio Guerriero

Foreword by John L. Allen, Jr.

D1225787

BOOKS & MEDIA

Boston

Library of Congress Cataloging-in-Publication Data

Benedict XVI, Pope, 1927–
  [Giovanni Paolo II. English]
  John Paul II : my beloved predecessor / Joseph Ratzinger (Benedict XVI) ;
edited by Elio Guerriero ; foreword by John L. Allen, Jr.— 1st North
American English ed.
    p. cm.
  ISBN 0-8198-3989-2 (pbk.)
  1. John Paul II, Pope, 1920–2005. I. Guerriero, Elio. II. Title.
  BX1378.5.B45513 2007
  282.092—dc22

                                    2007022124

Cover design by Rosana Usselmann

Cover photo: Pope John Paul II (l) during a meeting with Cardinal Joseph Ratzinger in Munich, Germany, 1980. © Frank Leonhardt/epa/Corbis

Chapters 1, 2, and Conclusion translated by Matthew Sherry
Chapters 3–7: Vatican translation

Original edition published in Italian by Edizioni San Paolo, Milan, Italy

Copyright © Libreria Editrice Vaticana, Edizioni San Paolo s.r.l. 2007— Piazza Soncino, 5-20092 Cinisello Balsamo (Milano)

First English Edition, 2007

Published by Pauline Books & Media, 50 Saint Paul's Avenue, Boston, MA 02130-3491. www.pauline.org.

Printed in the U.S.A.

Pauline Books & Media is the publishing house of the Daughters of St. Paul, an international congregation of women religious serving the Church with the communications media.

1 2 3 4 5 6 7 8 9   11 10 09 08 07

JOHN PAUL II

MY BELOVED PREDECESSOR

Contents

Foreword

In 1996, then-Cardinal Joseph Ratzinger sat down for a lengthy interview with the German journalist Peter Seewald, which eventually became the book *Salt of the Earth*. Near the end of their conversation, Seewald asked Ratzinger to explain Pope John Paul II's vision of the third millennium as a "new springtime of the human spirit." Ratzinger offered one of his legendarily lucid replies, condensing complex ideas into crystalline sentences. He explained that John Paul saw the first millennium as one of Christian unity, the second as one of division, and the third millennium as one of new unity, not just for Christianity but for the entire human family.

After having set out this grand vision, Ratzinger permitted himself a touch of skepticism: "At the moment," he observed wryly, "I do not yet see it approaching."

There, in a single phrase, lies the contrast between Karol Wojtyla the poet and mystic, and Joseph Ratzinger the academic and realist. Where Wojtyla always saw the status quo as a permeable membrane between the stirrings of the human spirit and the unbounded possibilities of God's grace, Ratzinger can be impatient with excogitations that seem divorced from concrete reality.

In important ways, these are two very different men. Had Wojtyla not become a priest, bishop, and pope, he would have been an actor; had Ratzinger not gone down the same path, he would have been a university professor. Wojtyla was at home on the stage, Ratzinger in a book-lined study. By the standards of pop culture, John Paul was also "hip," an adjective few would dare apply to Benedict XVI.

Among the jewels of this small collection edited by Elio Guerriero is a tribute prepared by Ratzinger in 1998, on the occasion of the twentieth anniversary of John Paul's election to the papacy. In passing, Ratzinger refers to the famous Eucharistic Congress in Bologna, Italy, in September 1997, when Bob Dylan and other rock stars performed for the pope and a crowd of youth.

Ratzinger cannot disguise that the event stretched his comfort zone: "There was reason to be skeptical—

I was then and, to some extent, still am," he writes, "and to question whether it was right to bring in these kinds of 'prophets.'" John Paul had no such reservations, even quoting Dylan that night to roars from his young audience. Another rock star, Bono of the Irish band U2, once allowed John Paul to playfully don his trademark sunglasses, upon which Bono pronounced him "history's first funky pontiff." It seems deeply improbable that anyone will nominate Benedict XVI as the second.

What, then, was the secret of their close collaboration and friendship over a quarter-century?

C. S. Lewis wrote that friendship is born when two people, however different from one another, see the same truth. That is undoubtedly the core of the symbiosis between Karol Wojtyla and Joseph Ratzinger, and between the pontificates of John Paul II and Benedict XVI. These two men were gripped by the same truth—or, better expressed, the same Truth, in the person of Jesus Christ, and in the company of the Church. That two such distinct personalities could work so closely together for so long, without any of the rivalries and power dynamics that typically accompany such partnerships (think Tony Blair and Gordon Brown, for example), says much about the selflessness of both.

Joseph Ratzinger enabled Karol Wojtyla to revolutionize the papal office, to be daring, and to "push the envelope," because he knew that Ratzinger would keep him grounded in tradition. Likewise, John Paul II taught the shy, cerebral Benedict XVI how to perform on the public stage, how to allow his own personality to infuse his office without ever overshadowing it, and how to reach out to others while sacrificing nothing of his own identity. Rather than exploiting one another's weaknesses, the two men admired and sought to emulate the other's strengths. The texts collected in this volume testify to Benedict XVI's efforts to do just that.

One passage not included by Guerriero deserves mention here. The morning after his election, Benedict XVI celebrated Mass with the cardinals in the Sistine Chapel, invoking his predecessor in startlingly personal terms: "It seems I can feel his strong hand squeezing mine," Benedict said. "I seem to see his smiling eyes and listen to his words, addressed to me especially at this moment: 'Do not be afraid!' " That tender image captures Benedict's depth of feeling better than any lengthy theological analysis.

Since this is a volume of texts by Benedict XVI about John Paul II, perhaps it is appropriate to close by giving voice instead to John Paul II, speaking about his friend and confidante who is now Benedict XVI. On the occasion of the fiftieth anniversary of Ratzinger's ordination to the priesthood in 2002, John Paul wrote him a letter, saying:

Your brilliant philosophical and, in particular, theological studies, and your precocious call to teaching roles in the most important German universities, should be seen in the perspective of faith. You expressed the intention that has always guided you in your commitment to study and teaching in the motto you chose on the occasion of your episcopal appointment: *Cooperatores veritatis*. The aim for which you have always striven, since your very first years as a priest, has been to serve the truth, seeking to know it ever more thoroughly and make it ever more widely known.[1]

After two years as Pope Benedict XVI, it's clear that this aim guides Joseph Ratzinger still...and that he still feels John Paul's strong hand holding his own. This small treasure of a book opens a window onto their striking, and deeply consequential, friendship.

JOHN L. ALLEN, JR.
May 2007

Preface

Benedict XVI has not written a history of John Paul II's pontificate, nor an essay on his predecessor's thought. With a gesture that is both simple and courageous, the new pope takes his place among the ranks of the faithful, among the admirers of John Paul II who wish to express their esteem and affection for him. And in order to foster the veneration that has emerged to accompany his memory, Benedict XVI is giving to John Paul's admirers writings that are primarily an invitation to venerate the Servant of God, to imitate his courage and faith, to persevere in prayer like him, despite the more or less burdensome responsibilities each of us must face. This book is limited to assembling the writings that Joseph Ratzinger/Benedict XVI expressly dedicated to the figure of his predecessor, while excluding the numerous event-specific references present in these documents and speeches. The material has been evenly divided into eight chapters: the first four contain texts that Joseph Ratzinger wrote as Prefect of the Congregation for the Doctrine of the Faith; the other four contain writings that followed his election to the See of Peter. The aim of this selection is twofold: to foster devotion to John Paul II, and to demonstrate the deep and tender friendship between the two most recent popes— something completely new in the history of the papacy and of great edification for the faithful.

The first text [*John Paul II: Unity of Mission and Person*], from 1998, is a tentative retrospective that the then-Cardinal Ratzinger compiled for the occasion of the twentieth anniversary of John Paul II's pontificate. While it is obviously not an exhaustive document, it nevertheless succeeds in capturing the new and charismatic way that Karol Wojtyla played out the ministry of the successor of Peter, so much so that the supposedly frosty Prefect of the Congregation for the Doctrine of the Faith seems almost on the verge of breaking into song. Of World Youth Day in Paris he writes: "...I have not found [anyone] who was not caught up in the atmosphere of this encounter in the faith. It had suddenly become a beautiful thing to be Christian" (p. 19).

The next two texts [*The Faith Is Humanity's Refuge* and *The Poetry of John Paul II*] cross the threshold of the new millennium, and approach the conclusion of John Paul II's ministry. The first text, from 2003, is an insightful interpretation of the magisterium of the Polish pope as expressed in his fourteen encyclicals. The dominant themes here are God and man. Between these two stand Jesus and the Church. Jesus Christ, the redeemer of man, is the path to the Father of mercy in the Spirit who is Lord and Giver of life. The Church, with its sacraments and teaching, is how Jesus speaks to man in every age, in order to remind him of his dignity. The second selection, also from 2003, is the presentation of the *Roman Triyptych,* a poetic text in which the elderly pope, with the help of Michelangelo's images in the Sistine Chapel, catches sight of the river of life that first descends and then rises back up toward its goal. Ratzinger writes:

> The contemplation of the Last Judgment in the epilogue of the second panel is perhaps the part of the *Triptych* that most moves the reader. From the pope's interior eye emerges, in a fresh way, the memory of the conclaves of August and October 1978.... The word "con-clave" makes one think of the keys, of the patrimony of the keys handed to Peter. To place these keys in the right hands: this is the immense responsibility of those days. (p. 50)

Two years later, in 2005, John Paul II, after living out the Paschal Mystery for us, "stood at the window of the Father's house" (Funeral Mass, April 8). From there, he followed the election of his former co-worker, and, on August 18, stood with him on the boat that brought him up the Rhine to meet with the young people gathered in Cologne. And Benedict did not fail to remember him:

> Today, as I arrived in Cologne to take part with you in the twentieth World Youth Day, I naturally recall with deep gratitude the Servant of God so greatly loved by us all, Pope John Paul II, who had the inspired idea of calling young people from all over the world. (p. 69)

One year after the death of the Polish pontiff, in the three messages dedicated to his memory (the Angelus and Rosary on April 2, and the homily on the following day), Benedict XVI sought to encapsulate the life and evangelical witness of the great pontiff. He wrote:

> With his words and gestures, the dear John Paul II never tired of pointing out to the world that if a person allows himself to be embraced by Christ, he does not repress the riches of his humanity; if he adheres to Christ with all his heart, he will never lack anything. On the contrary, the encounter with Christ makes our lives more impassioned. (p. 81)

The following month, in May 2006, Benedict XVI was in Poland, a pilgrim in the footsteps of John Paul. He dedicated three substantial addresses to his beloved predecessor: in Warsaw, Wadowice, and

Kraków. In Wadowice, recalling the baptismal font where the future pontiff's life of grace began, he said:

> The way of an authentically Christian life equals faithfulness to the promises of holy Baptism. The watchword of this pilgrimage: "Stand firm in your faith," finds in this place its concrete dimension that can be expressed with the exhortation: "Stand firm in the observance of your baptismal promises." A witness of just such a faith—of whom this place speaks in a very special way—is the Servant of God John Paul II. (p. 98)

The path we have just traced out is a journey of spiritual friendship. This communion in the faith, moreover, like that of many saints, is a way of attraction that leads people to Christ, invites them to open themselves to the One who deepens and fulfills man's life. The vigor of Wojtyla's faith encountered the rationality of the servant of the Lord's vineyard [Ratzinger], ready to give the reasons for Christian hope. They worked together—and still do—in service of the truth that is the love of the Father made known by his Son, Jesus Christ.

ELIO GUERRIERO

PART I

JOSEPH RATZINGER ON POPE JOHN PAUL II

1998–2005

CHAPTER I

John Paul II:
Unity of Mission and Person

TWENTY YEARS OF HISTORY

As pope for twenty years, he [Pope John Paul II] has undoubtedly met personally with more people from all over the world than anyone else. There are countless people whose hands he has shaken, with whom he has spoken, with whom he has prayed, and whom he has blessed.

If his lofty office can create distance, his personal magnetism instead creates closeness. Even simple, poor, uneducated people do not get the impression that he is above them, unreachable, or intimidating— the feelings that so often strike those who find themselves in the antechambers of the powerful. And then, when one has personal contact with him, it is as if he is an old acquaintance, as if one were speaking with a family member or friend. The title "Father" (Papa)[2] no longer seems a title, but the expression of the real relationship one truly feels in his presence.

Everyone knows John Paul II: his face, his distinctive way of moving and speaking; his immersion in prayer, his spontaneous joy. Some of his words have engraved themselves indelibly on our memories, beginning with the passionate appeal that he issued at the beginning of his pontificate: "Throw wide open the doors to Christ, do not be afraid of him!" Or these words: "Life cannot be a trial run; love cannot be a trial run!" An entire pontificate is condensed in words like these. It is as if he wanted to open pathways to Christ all over, as if he wanted to make accessible to all the entryway to true life, to true love.

If, like Paul, he is found constantly and untiringly on a journey "to the ends of the earth," if he wants to be near to all and to lose no opportunity to proclaim the Good News, it is not for promotional reasons or out of a thirst for popularity, but because in him are realized the Apostle's words: "The love of Christ urges us on" (2 Cor 5:14). Being near him, one realizes that he cares about people because he cares about God.

One gets to know John Paul II best by concelebrating Mass with him, by letting oneself be drawn into the intense silence of his prayer, more than by analyzing his books or speeches. By participating in his prayer, one moves beyond words and into his very being. Continued reflection in this vein helps one to understand why, although he is a great intellectual with his own significant voice in the modern world's cultural dialogue, he has also maintained a simplicity that permits him to communicate with every single person.

There is another element of this great capacity for inclusion that distinguishes the Polish pope: his having exchanged the classical "we" of the pontifical style for the personal and immediate "I" of the writer and orator. Such a stylistic revolution should not be underestimated. At first glance it may seem the obvious elimination of an antiquated usage no longer applicable in our time. But one must not forget that this "we" was not a mere formula of rhetorical courtesy.

When the pope speaks, he does not speak in his own name. At that moment, in the final analysis, the private theories or opinions that he has elaborated over the course of his life count for nothing, as refined as they may be intellectually. The pope does not speak as an erudite individual, with his private "I," or, so to speak, as a lone observer of humanity's spiritual history. When he speaks, he draws from the "we" of the whole Church's faith, behind which the "I" must disappear.

In this context, I am reminded of the great humanist Pope Pius II, Enea Silvio Piccolomini, who, drawing from the "we" of his pontifical magisterium, sometimes found he had to speak in contradiction to the theories of the savvy humanist he had once been. When he was told about these contradictions, he usually replied, *"Eneum reicite, Pium recipite"* ("Leave Enea alone, and take Pius the pope"). In a certain sense, then, it is no small matter if the "I" replaces the "we."

But those who make the effort to study attentively all the writings of Pope John Paul II will quickly realize that this pope is very much able to distinguish between the personal opinions of Karol Wojtyla and his magisterial teaching as pope. However, he also recognizes that the two are not mutually exclusive, but reflect a single personality imbued with the faith of the Church. The "I," the personality, has entered fully into the service of the "we." He has not debased the "we" to the subjective level of private opinion, but has simply bestowed upon it the density of a personality entirely shaped by this "we," completely dedicated to its service.

I believe that such a fusion between the "we" and the "I," developed by living the faith and reflecting upon it, is the essential foundation of this pope's allure. This fusion permits him to live his sacred ministry in a completely free and natural way; it permits him to be completely himself as pope, without having to be afraid of letting his office slide too far into subjectivism.

But how did this unity come about? How does a personal journey of faith, thought, and life arrive so deeply within the heart of the Church? This question goes far beyond simple biographical curiosity—precisely because such an "identification" with the Church, without any veil of hypocrisy or schizophrenia, seems impossible to many people today who are in anguish over their faith.

In theology it has become, in the meantime, almost a fashionable form of flirtation to maintain a critical distance from the Church, and to make it clear to the reader that he, the theologian, is not so naïve, so uncritical and servile as to place his thought entirely at the service of this faith. In this way the faith is devalued, and the hasty proposals of these theologians take nothing constructive from it and die off as quickly as they were born. This leads to the rebirth of a great desire not only to reconsider the faith intellectually and loyally, but also to be able to live it in a new way.

Wojtyla's study of philosophy

Karol Wojtyla's vocation matured while he was working in a chemical factory, during the horrors of the war and the occupation. He himself has described this period of four years in the world of labor as the most decisive period of his life. It was in this context that he studied philosophy, learning it painstakingly from books—and philosophical knowledge at first seemed like an impenetrable jungle. His point of departure was philology—the love of language—combined with the artistic application of language, as a representation of reality, in a new form of theater. This is how the distinctive form of "philosophy" characteristic of the current pope[3] emerged. It is a way of thinking in dialogue with the concrete, founded upon the great tradition, but always in search of confirmation in present reality. It is a form of thought that springs from an artist's gaze and, at the same time, is guided by a pastor's care. And it is offered to man, to show him the way.

I think it is worthwhile to spend a few moments reviewing in chronological order the crucial authors among whom he set off on the path of his formation. The first, as he himself recounts in his interview with André Frossard, was [the author of] an introductory manual of metaphysics.[4] Although other students tried only to comprehend in some way the overall logic of the conceptual structure presented in the text and to fix it in their minds for their exams, he instead began the struggle for a real comprehension, for a grasp of the relationship between concept and experience. And after two months of hard work, the "light" came on: "I understood the deep meaning of everything that I had only experienced and glimpsed before."

Then came his encounter with Max Scheler and phenomenology. Following endless controversies about the limitations and possibilities of human knowledge, this philosophical approach sought to look again at phenomena simply as they appear, in their variety and richness. This precision in seeing, this comprehension of man beginning not from abstractions and theoretical principles, but seeking to grasp his reality with love, was—and remains—decisive for the pope's thought.

Finally, he discovered fairly early on, before his vocation to the priesthood, the work of Saint John of the Cross, through which the word of interiority, "of the soul ripened by grace," was opened to him.

All of these elements—metaphysical, mystical, phenomenological, and aesthetic—combined to open his eyes to the many dimensions of reality, and they became in the end a single unified perception capable of meeting and understanding all phenomena by transcending them. The crisis of post-conciliar theology is, to a large extent, the crisis of its philosophical foundations.

The form of philosophy presented in the theological schools was lacking in perceptual richness; it lacked phenomenology, and the mystical dimension was missing. And when basic philosophical principles are unclear, theology finds the ground beginning to give way beneath its feet. That is because it is no longer clear to what extent man truly understands reality, and on what basis he can think and speak. So, it seems to me a disposition of Providence that, at this time, a "philosopher" has risen to the See of Peter, a man who does not simply take his philosophy from a textbook, but exerts the effort necessary to meet the challenge of reality and of man's quest and questioning.

The theme of Karol Wojtyla's philosophy was, and is, man. His scholarly interest was always heavily influenced by his vocation as a pastor. This helps explain why his involvement in drafting the conciliar Constitution on the Church in the Modern World[5]— a document fundamentally shaped by a concern for man—became a decisive experience for the future pope. "Man is the way for the Church." This maxim, so concrete and radical in its profundity, has always been at the center of his thought, which is one and the same with his action. The result is that the question of moral theology has become the center of his theological interests.

This was another important human predisposition in terms of taking on the tasks of the Church's supreme pastor—because the crisis in philosophical orientation is manifested above all, from the theological point of view, as a crisis in the norms of moral theology. This is where the link between philosophy and theology is found, the bridge between rational inquiry about man and the task of theology—and this is so evident a bond that it simply cannot be set aside. Wherever the old metaphysics collapses, there also the Commandments lose their internal cohesion, and a great temptation arises to reduce them merely to the level of history and culture.

Wojtyla had learned from Scheler to investigate, with a degree of human sensitivity previously unknown, the essence of virginity, matrimony, motherhood and fatherhood, the language of the body— and, therefore, the essence of love. He incorporated into his thought the new discoveries of personalism, and this led him to the understanding that the body itself speaks, that creation speaks and shows us the way we should go. Modern thought has opened up a new dimension for moral theology, and Wojtyla has grasped this through a continual mining of his reflection and experience, of his pastoral and intellectual vocation, and he has grasped this in its unity with the great themes of tradition.

Man is the way for the Church

There was still another important element for this journey of life and thought, for the unity of experience, thought, and faith. This man's battle did not take place entirely in a more or less private sphere, solely within the walls of a factory or a seminary. It was, rather, surrounded by the flames of major historical events—Wojtyla's presence in the factory was the result of the arrest of his university professors.

His peaceful academic studies were interrupted and replaced by a grueling apprenticeship in the midst of an oppressed people. His attendance at Cardinal Sapieha's major seminary was in itself an act of resistance.

Thus the questions of freedom, human dignity, and rights, the political responsibilities conferred by faith, did not enter the thoughts of the young theologian as merely theoretical problems. Facing these was the very real and concrete necessity of that historical moment. Once again the particular situation in Poland, at the intersection of East and West, had become that country's destiny.

The pope's critics often observe that, as a native of Poland, he really knows only the traditional and sentimental piety of his country, and thus cannot fully comprehend the complicated questions of the Western world. There could not be a more ridiculous observation, which betrays a complete ignorance of history. One need only read the encyclical *Slavorum Apostoli* to get the sense that the pope needed precisely this Polish heritage to be able to take a variety of cultures into account.

Because Poland is a point of intersection for civilizations—and in particular for the Germanic, Roman, Slavic, and Greco-Byzantine traditions—the question of intercultural dialogue is in many ways more pressing in Poland than elsewhere. And therefore this very pope is a truly ecumenical and missionary pope, one providentially prepared, even in this sense, to confront the questions of the period following the Second Vatican Council.

Let us return again to the pope's pastoral and anthropological interests. "Man is the way for the Church." The authentic meaning of this often misunderstood assertion in the encyclical *Redeemer of Man* can be truly understood if we recall that for the pope, "man" in the full sense is Jesus Christ. His passion for man has nothing to do with a self-sufficient anthropocentrism. Here, anthropocentrism is open toward heaven. Every form of anthropocentrism that aims at removing God as an obstacle to man has for some time been turned into indifference on the part of man and toward man. Man can no longer consider himself the center of the world. And he is afraid of himself because of his own destructive power.

When man is placed at the center to the exclusion of God, the overall balance is upset—and then it is that the passage in the Letter to the Romans (8:19, 21–22) holds true, where it says that the world was dragged into suffering and sorrow by man; ruined in Adam, it has since then been waiting for the coming of the children of God, for their liberation. Precisely because the pope has man at heart, he wants to open the doors to Christ. This is because it is only with the coming of Christ that the children of Adam can become children of God, and man and creation can enter into their freedom. The pope's anthropocentrism is, therefore, in its most profound depths, theocentrism.

If his first encyclical appears to be entirely centered upon man, his three great encyclicals naturally come together into a grand Trinitarian triptych: for the pope, anthropocentrism is theocentrism because the source of his pastoral activity is prayer, thus his experience of man comes in communion with God, and from this comes his understanding.

The unity of mystery and person in the figure of the pope

One final observation: the pope's deep love for Mary is certainly a legacy from his homeland of Poland, but his Marian encyclical[6] shows how much this Marian piety has been biblically deepened in him through prayer and life. In the same way that his philosophy was made more concrete and lively through phenomenology—or through gazing at reality as it appears—so also the pope's relationship with Christ does not remain in the abstract of the great dogmatic truths, but becomes a concrete, human encounter with the Lord in all his reality. Therefore it logically becomes an encounter with his Mother, in whom believing Israel and the praying Church become one person. Once again, it is always and only through this concrete closeness—in which the mystery of Christ is seen in all the richness of his divine-human fullness—that a relationship with the Lord receives its warmth and vitality. And, naturally, the fact that this response of faith has taken form forever in a woman, in Mary, reflects back on the entire image of the human person.

What do I want to say with all of this? My aim is to demonstrate the unity between mystery and person in the figure of Pope John Paul II. He truly is "identified" with the Church, and can therefore be its voice. All of this is not said to glorify a human creature, but to demonstrate that believing does not extinguish thought, and it does not need to place the experience of our time in parentheses. On the contrary: only faith gives thought its openness and gives experience its meaning. Man does not become free through isolation, but by discovering the greater context to which he belongs.

After the blossoming of the first ten years, distracted observers had formed the conviction that the second decade of John Paul II's pontificate could not bring much of anything new. But those who make even a minimal effort to look a little closer will discover that this pontificate continues to hold surprises, and that even the most recent years have their own particular fruitfulness, their own distinctive characteristics. Still, it is true that the early enthusiasm for this youthfully energetic pope, his openness to the questions of our time, his courage before the unexpected, his gusto for life, his breaking of the usual rules and forms—all of that enthusiasm has dried up.

There have been times of harsh criticism; here and there, signs of disinterest have emerged toward the words of this tireless pilgrim who has traveled over all the continents. And yet, he still attracts surprisingly large audiences, and his words and gestures continue to make themselves felt and heard, casting out resentment and touching hearts.

This has happened on many of his most recent travels: some had said that no one cared anymore about this old man, and that his message was no longer relevant. But then, upon his arrival, his personality proved stronger than all the prejudices that had been raised against him. I think, for example, of

his latest visit to France [in 1996]. The circumstances
were rather difficult. The memory of the baptism of
Clovis, which was to be commemorated as the beginning of French history, had suddenly cast the French
into a bitter conflict over their history. Linking Clovis
to the inception of France seemed to many a clerical
usurpation of this history, with a glory they thought
consisted in the fact that it must be read according to
a "secular" hermeneutic.

Within the Church, it was asked whether it was
right to put the pope in the middle of such con-
tentious disputes, in which he would have been uni-
laterally bound to certain historical images. But as
soon as the pope arrived, this dispute seemed to have
been completely set aside. He spoke with such simplicity, from the very heart of the faith, touching
intimately upon the issues that trouble us in these
times, that those present found themselves united in
a great celebration of faith, and those who watched
from a distance showed a new attitude of reflection.
On the occasion of that same visit, the pope—who
was depicted as a strict moralist and as the herald of
a sternness that ignored human needs—found words
full of understanding for those at the margins of
society and at the margins of the Church, for the
downtrodden and suffering, for the discouraged and
abandoned. He spoke so as to impart faith and create

a desire for mutual support and welcome—which is, after all, the real heart of Christian morality.

The Church's reality is palpable in John Paul II

An important feature of the most recent years of Pope John Paul II's pontificate must be mentioned at this point: he who speaks in this way to the masses is himself a man of suffering. Pain is inscribed upon his face. His body is stooped, he moves with difficulty, he needs the pastoral staff of the papal ministry—surmounted by a cross—as a cane to support his weight. He leans upon the cross, upon the crucifix. So we might have expected that his appeal to young people, which has emerged more clearly each year, would have diminished. What can this sick, suffering, tired old man say, who in moments of physical fatigue speaks with visible weariness?

This preoccupation circulated in a particular way before the most recent large gathering of young people in Paris.[7] Many newspapers took it for granted that participation would be disappointing. But the crowds that gathered so far exceeded even the most optimistic forecasts that serious organizational problems resulted. And even though the heat played its part in making the organization of the encounter difficult, all of the participants lived the celebration as an unforgettable time of joy, in which one could finally begin to experience what life is, what life can and should be.

I have had the chance to talk about these days with many people who participated in them, including those who had come with strongly skeptical attitudes. Yet I have not found a single person who was not caught up in the atmosphere of this encounter in the faith. It had suddenly become a beautiful thing to be Christian. Those present experienced that it is wonderful to pray together, to keep silent together, to receive the sacrament of Penance, and thus find reconciliation with oneself, with God, and with others; that it is beautiful to take part in the Eucharist, and thus feel the Lord's presence.

I believe that one absolutely cannot fail to discover in this event the salvific power of the presence of the living God. Obviously, many elements contributed to its success, but truly essential for these days was the fact that the pope made palpable the reality of the Church, the reality of the mystery, something that goes well beyond human capacities and abilities. It was precisely the suffering pope who was in a unique way a window into the presence of something greater.

He was at the center, yet the center was not his own person, but rather Christ, whom he represented. The Pauline expression "I will boast all the more gladly of my weaknesses" (2 Cor 12:9) took on greater clarity for me there. The Apostle meant to say that he himself, with his own talents and strengths, was completely unequipped for the greatness of the task that had been entrusted to him and that he had undertaken. But it was precisely in this way that it became clear that he was not constructing something on his own, that in the end it was not at all he himself who was building the universal Church, but that his strength came from somewhere else.

John Paul II's life under the sign of the cross

The same thing struck me on the occasion of the Eucharistic Congress in Bologna:[8] the pope seemed tired, fatigued. At that very moment the stars, Bob Dylan and others whose names I don't remember, arrived for the young people. They had a message completely different from the one for which the pope labors. There was reason to be skeptical—I was then and, to some extent, still am—and to question whether it was right to bring in these kinds of "prophets." But all of a sudden their message seemed weak and outdated when the pope put aside the hand-written text in front of him and began to speak to the young people from his heart, saying things to them that, at first glance, one would not have the courage to say. He spoke to them of the meaning of failure, sacrifice, the acceptance of suffering, the cross.

On that occasion, the pope used no worn-out, empty religious formulas. Someone remarked that—as in the words for priestly ordination—he had placed "his life under the sign of the cross," and that this had made him wise.

He [John Paul II] put his finger on what the entertainment industry and the modern way of life ignore completely—and yet is the question that each one of us personally faces. It is this: as long as I encounter things that are beneath me, my highest faculties lie dormant—and in some way, each one of us realizes this.

It seems to me that it is precisely in the pope's physical and spiritual suffering, which no one can ignore, that one can find a particular message in this second half of his pontificate.

Today, everything is aimed at the effort for results and at practicality. The man of politics must come across as youthful in order to seem electable; the modern managerial professions presuppose a good physical appearance. Strangely, in a society that is visibly aging, the cult of youth continues to grow. Sickness and old age must stay hidden as much as possible. The pope does not hide them; he cannot and does not want to hide them. It is just in this way that he carries out an important service for us. Old age, too, has its own message, and suffering has its dignity and its salvific power.

I cannot fail to recall how the pope spoke to us on the occasion of the Mass for the African synod, which brought him such great joy, while he was in the hospital after falling in the bathroom and breaking his hip. He had earlier visited the "Weeping Madonna" in Syracuse, and began his remarks to us by speaking about this event. No sermon that he might have preached to us in good health could have touched us in the same way. The "Weeping Madonna" stood for all the tears of the innocent, whom no one is able to console. How many tears have fallen in these years in Africa; we think of Rwanda, of Mozambique, of Nigeria, of Guinea-Bissau, and of many other countries. The suffering pope spoke on behalf of the suffering in this world, and, in a completely unexpected way and with distressing realism, he spoke of the sufferings of Africa, becoming in this way the credible herald of divine compassion, capable of credibly soliciting human compassion.

A teaching of extraordinary density

In the second decade of his pontificate, too, the pope gave us a teaching of extraordinary density and intensity, characterized by many unique features in comparison with his first encyclicals. His letters from the first years of his pontificate are very deeply marked by his personal reflection and meditation;

above all, the great Trinitarian triptych—*Redemptor Hominis, Dives in Misericordia, Dominum et Vivificantem*—conveys the pope's unmistakable voice. In the magisterial documents of the second decade one also finds the characteristic features of his thought, which provide their direction and style. But these are magisterial texts, which go to the depths, on the one hand, with great care, to make their own the questions of the present time, and, on the other hand, evaluate these in light of the fullness of tradition, teaching how to unite continuity and development. Above all I think of the great encyclical on the foundations of moral theology (*Veritatis Splendor*), which we can easily consider a groundbreaking document, a milestone in the updating of Christianity's moral message, which speaks to the conscience of people well beyond the circle of believers. Or there is the encyclical on the missions, *Redemptoris Missio,* that recalls the Church's missionary task in the context of contemporary interreligious dialogue, illustrating the correct relationship between dialogue and proclamation. I think also of *Evangelium Vitae,* which is a celebration of life in the context of the culture of death, in which an unhealthy desire for life seeks support in death, presenting as good works the homicidal acts of abortion and euthanasia.

In some cases, these texts have found a better reception among thinkers outside of the Church than among some of the representatives of Catholic theology. It may be that many non-Christian thinkers feel the seriousness and urgency of humanity's personal crisis far more intimately than some Catholic theologians do; they feel that the destruction of moral conscience constitutes a greater threat to humanity than nuclear energy or disease. Or a better way of putting it may be that they believe that both the atomic bomb and injustice, which increasingly produces hunger and misery, threaten us only because moral failings have led us to this abuse of human potential—and will continue to feed this abuse if there is no decisive move in the other direction.

In this encyclical, the pope has developed a view of morality that is sufficiently broad and deep to make its own the moral wisdom of the great religious traditions and of human reason—the appeal to reason, to its capacity to grasp the lesson of the Creator from creation, is a fundamental aspect of this document. But it also brings to light the new moral certainty and concreteness that have entered the world through Christ and have become a source of strength for all humanity when believers live them in such a way that they are plain for all to see. The autumn of this year[9] saw the publication of the encyclical *Fides et Ratio*, which focuses on the relationship between faith and reason—and, as we have already seen, this was also in the background of *Veritatis Splendor.* The new encyclical, then, deals just as much with the public responsibility of believers as it does with communicating the faith. It is a document that truly deserves attentive reading.

Everything points back to God:
looking forward to the year 2000

I would like to mention another series of texts from this decade. Ever since his first encyclical, published shortly after the beginning of his pontificate, the pope has called attention to the approach of the year 2000, speaking of this almost as a new Advent. The Church, not looking behind but straight ahead, goes forth with the Christ who has already come, to meet the Lord who is yet to come. The day that commemorates the Lord's incarnation is surely a day of hope for the pontiff. Christ is alive. He can and wants to renew the world in the midst of all its crises, that the world may open itself to the reign of God.

For the pope, looking toward the year 2000 means looking toward the living power of the Risen One, toward him who provides more than we need. But it is also a challenge, a dare to go forward to meet him—and this is the central idea of three important documents in recent years. The first is the encyclical on ecumenism, *Ut Unum Sint.* From the beginning, the pope has felt the division within Christianity as a wound that touches him very personally, to the point of physical pain. He therefore considers it his duty to do whatever he can to turn the tide toward unity. For this reason, he has poured all of his passion for ecumenism into this document. In some passages, one almost seems to hear a cry for help, a call for support so that he might become a servant of unity, and that the third millennium, after the divisions of the second, may bring an era of renewed fellowship.

Besides this great encyclical, there is another ecumenical document by the pope that has remained in obscurity for too long: the apostolic letter *Orientale Lumen,* in which the Slavic pope demonstrates the depth of his love for the churches of the East.

> A pope, son of a Slav people, is particularly moved by the call of those peoples to whom the two saintly brothers Cyril and Methodius went. They were a glorious example of apostles of unity who were able to proclaim Christ in their search for communion between East and West amid the difficulties that sometimes set the two worlds against one another.[10]

This letter by the pope represents a small but precious *summa* of Eastern spirituality, a magisterial document that could help our Western spirituality, with its strong tendency toward rationalism, to rediscover the heritage of the East and to draw closer to it, beginning with its interior practice as part of the spiritual life.

Finally, I would like to call attention to the apostolic letter *Tertio Millennio Adveniente,* explicitly dedicated to the Jubilee of the year 2000, in which the pope offers a sober yet magnificent explanation of this celebration, while also outlining a detailed pastoral program for its preparation and realization. One could say that this letter is a handbook for the new evangelization that is so dear to the Holy Father's heart. The ideas of penance and joy are intermingled here in a surprising way. While on the one hand the entire text is dominated by the theme of God as developed in the Church's Trinitarian faith in the Father, Son, and Holy Spirit, on the other hand this theme, so fundamental for every human being, is shown to be very concretely interwoven with the dispositions of faith, hope, and love, and with the sacraments of Baptism, Confirmation, Penance, and the Eucharist. This is how a way is made for an ecclesiology in which everything points back to God, and God himself becomes our pathway through the sacraments of the living Church.

Today even critics feel with ever greater clarity that the crisis of our times consists in the "crisis of God," in the disappearance of God from the horizon of human history. The Church's response can only be to speak less about itself and always more about God, to bear witness to him, and to be a door to him.

This is the true meaning of John Paul II's pontificate, as is becoming increasingly evident with the passing years. This modest attempt at homage will, therefore, end with Aaron's words of blessing, which the new liturgy offers as the reading at the beginning of the New Year, on the first day of the year, which has become the feast of the Mother of God, whom John Paul II so greatly venerates and loves:

> The Lord bless him and keep him;
> the Lord make his face to shine upon him
>   and be gracious to him;
> the Lord lift up his countenance upon him
>   and give him peace (cf. Num 6:24–26).

Chapter II

The Faith
Is Humanity's Refuge

The Fourteen Encyclicals of John Paul II

The encyclicals of John Paul II should first of all be divided according to their common themes. In the first place, we should recall the Trinitarian triptych of the years 1979 to 1986, which includes the encyclicals *Redemptor Hominis, Dives in Misericordia,* and *Dominum et Vivificantem.* To the decade 1981 to 1991 belong the three social encyclicals: *Laborem Exercens, Sollicitudo Rei Socialis,* and *Centesimus Annus.* Then there are the encyclicals that deal with ecclesiological themes: *Slavorum Apostoli* (1985), *Redemptoris Missio* (1990), and *Ut Unum Sint* (1995). The pope's last encyclical, *Ecclesia de Eucharistia* (2003), can also be assigned to the area of ecclesiology, as can, in a certain sense, the Marian encyclical *Redemptoris Mater* (1987). Already in his very first encyclical, the pope had closely linked the theme of the Church as mother with that of the Mother of the Church, expanding these into the areas of history, theology, and pneumatology:

> Above all, I implore Mary, the heavenly Mother of the Church, to be so good as to devote herself to this prayer of humanity's new Advent, together with us who make up the Church, that is to say the Mystical Body of her only Son. I hope that through this prayer we shall be able to receive the Holy Spirit coming upon us (cf. Acts 1:8) and thus become Christ's witnesses "to the end of the earth" (ibid).[11]

For the pope, Mariology brings together all of the great themes of the faith; not one of his encyclicals ends without acknowledging the Mother of the Lord. And finally, we have three great doctrinal texts that can be assigned to the realm of anthropology: *Veritatis Splendor* (1993), *Evangelium Vitae* (1995), and *Fides et Ratio* (1998).

The Trinitarian encyclicals

The first encyclical, *Redemptor Hominis,* is the most personal, the point of departure for all the other encyclicals. It would be easy to demonstrate that all of the later themes are mentioned here: the theme of truth and the link between truth and freedom is addressed with all the importance that it has in a world that wants freedom, but that considers the truth a pretense and the opposite of liberty. The pope's passion for ecumenism also emerges in this first magisterial document. The great highlights of the Eucharistic encyclical[12]—Eucharist and sacrifice, sacrifice and redemption, Eucharist and penance— are already present in broad outlines. The imperative "You shall not kill"—the central theme of *Evangelium Vitae*—is shouted out loudly to the world. As we have already seen, Christianity's direction toward the future is linked to the Marian theme—so typical of the pope. For the pope, the Church's connection to Christ is not a link to the past, not a looking back, but rather a bond with He Who Is, and who is and who gives the future, who invites the Church to open itself to a new era of faith. The pope's personal involvement, his hope, and even his profound desire that the Lord grant us a new day of faith and fullness of life, a new Pentecost, becomes evident when the invocation bursts forth from him: "The present-day Church seems to repeat with ever greater fervor and with holy insistence: 'Come, Holy Spirit!' Come! Come!"[13]

All of these themes, as we have already stated, which foreshadow the pope's entire magisterial work, are held together by a vision we must try to identify at least in its fundamental direction. During the retreat that he preached as Archbishop of Kraków in 1976 to Paul VI and the Roman Curia, he recounted how during the first years after World War II the Polish Catholic intellectuals had initially sought to refute, contrary to the official doctrine of Marxist materialism, the absolute dominance of the material. But very early on, the center of the debate shifted: it was no longer a question of the philosophical basis of the natural sciences (as important as this theme may be), but rather of anthropology. The question had become: Who is man? The anthropological question is not a mere philosophical theory about man, but it has an essential character. Behind it lies the question of redemption. How can man live? Who has the answer to the eminently concrete question about man? Who can teach us how to live: materialism, Marxism, or Christianity? The anthropological question is, therefore, a scientific and rational question, but at the same time it is also a pastoral question. How can we show people the way of life? And how can we make it clear to nonbelievers as well that their questions are our questions, and that, in the face of man's dilemma both then and now, Peter was right when he said to the Lord: "Lord, to whom can we go? You have the words of eternal life" (Jn 6:68)?

Philosophy, the pastoral ministry, and the Church's faith all merge in this anthropological dynamic.

God the Son

In his first encyclical John Paul II has, so to speak, summed up the fruit of his journey thus far as shepherd of the Church and as a thinker of our time. His first encyclical revolves around the question of man. The expression "man...is the primary and fundamental way for the Church"[14] has become a sort of motto. Yet, in citing this, we very often forget that shortly before the pope said, "Jesus Christ is the chief way for the Church. He himself is our way 'to the Father's house' (cf. Jn 14:1ff.) and is the way to each man."[15] Consequently even the phrase about man as the primary way for the Church continues like this: "the way traced out by Christ himself, the way that leads invariably through the mystery of the Incarnation and the Redemption."[16] For the pope, anthropology and Christology are inseparable. Who man is and where he must go to find life is precisely what was made visible in Christ. This Christ is not only an image of human existence, an example of how one must live, but he also "in a certain way united himself with each man."[17] He reaches us from the inside, at the root of our existence, thus becoming, from within, the way for every man. He breaks through the isolation of the ego; he is the guarantee of the inde-structible dignity of every individual, and at the same time it is he who overcomes individualism by establishing the unity for which man's entire nature longs.

For the pope, anthropocentrism is at the same time Christocentrism, and vice versa. Contrary to the opinion that only through primitive humanity (start-ing from below, so to speak) can human nature be explained, the pope maintains that only by beginning with the perfect man can one understand who man is, and only from this point of view can one glimpse the way of being human. In this context, he might have recalled these words from Teilhard de Chardin:

> The scientific solution of the human problem is in no way offered exclusively by the study of fossils, but by attentive observation of the characteristics and potential of the man of today, who will deter-mine the man of tomorrow.

Naturally, John Paul II goes well beyond this diagno-sis: ultimately we can know who man is only by look-ing at him who completely fulfills the nature of man, who is the image of God—he, the Son of God, God from God and light from light. Thus it perfectly cor-responds to the intrinsic orientation of the first encyclical that, in the unfolding of the papal magis-terium, it grew to form a Trinitarian triptych with the other two encyclicals. The question of man cannot be separated from the question of God. Guardini's statement that only the person who knows God can know man finds clear confirmation in this fusion of anthropology with the question of God.

God the Father

Let's take a further look at the other two panels of this Trinitarian triptych. The theme of God the Father appears, in a manner of speaking, hidden under the title *Dives in Misericordia*. One may well believe that the inspiration for this theme came to the pope from his devotion to Sister Faustina Kowalska of Kraków, whom he later elevated to the glory of the altar. This holy woman's great desire was to put the mercy of God at the center of Christian faith and life. Through the strength of her spiritual life, she brought the unique message of Christianity to light in our own time, marked by the ruthlessness of its ideologies. Suffice it to recall that even Seneca—an intellectual of the ancient Roman world, who was in many ways fairly close to Christianity—once said, "Compassion is a weakness, a disease." A thousand years later, Bernard of Clairvaux, in the spirit of the Church Fathers, came up with his marvelous formula: "God cannot suffer, but he can pity." I think it is wonderful that the pope has arranged his encyclical on God the Father under the theme of divine mercy. The first chapter heading in the encyclical is "He Who

Sees Me Sees the Father" (Jn 14:9). Seeing Christ means seeing the merciful God. It is noteworthy that this encyclical contains a three-page digression on the Old Testament terminology relating to the divine mercy. In this section there is an explanation of the word *rahmin,* which comes from the word *rehem* (womb), and confers the characteristics of maternal love upon the mercy of God. The other focal point of the encyclical is its profound interpretation of the parable of the Prodigal Son, in which the image of the Father shines forth in all its greatness and beauty.

God the Holy Spirit

We still must speak about the encyclical on the Holy Spirit, in which the themes of truth and conscience emerge. According to the pope, the true and proper gift of the Holy Spirit is "the gift of the truth of conscience and the gift of the certainty of redemption."[18] So at the root of sin is deceit, the rejection of the truth: "Disobedience, as the original dimension of sin, means the rejection of this source [the divine law], through man's claim to become an independent and exclusive source for deciding about good and evil."[19] The fundamental perspective of *Veritatis Splendor* already appears quite plainly here. It is clear that the pope, in the encyclical on the Holy Spirit, does not stop at diagnosing the danger of our state, but lances the wound in order to open the way to healing. In conversion, weariness of conscience is transformed by the healing power of love, which knows how to suffer: "The hidden giver of this saving power is the Holy Spirit...."[20]

The social encyclicals

I have lingered—perhaps too long—over the Trinitarian triptych because it contains the complete program for the later encyclicals, connecting them all to faith in God. Unfortunately, I can dedicate to the other encyclicals just a few sketchy notes. The three great social encyclicals apply the pope's anthropology to the social problems of our age. He emphasizes the supremacy of man over the means of production, of labor over capital, of ethics over technology. At the center is the dignity of man, who is always an end and never a means; it is starting from here that the pope clarifies the great questions of contemporary society, in contrast with both Marxism and liberalism.[21]

The ecclesial encyclicals

The ecclesiological encyclicals deserve detailed attention that I cannot provide here. If *Ecclesia de Eucharistia* considers the Church from within and from on high—and thus grasps its ability to create communion, if *Redemptoris Mater* deals with the prefiguring of the Church in Mary and with the mystery of her maternity, the other three encyclicals in this group present the two great areas of relationship in which the Church lives. Ecumenical dialogue—as the search for the unity of the baptized according to the Lord's command, according to the intrinsic logic of the faith, which God has given the world as a force for unity—is the first area of relationship that the pope, with all the power of his passion for ecumenism, brings to the Church's awareness with *Ut Unum Sint.* *Slavorum Apostoli* is another ecumenical text of particular beauty. This document deals with the relationship between East and West, but it also shows the connection between faith and culture, and the capacity to create a culture of faith, which delves into its own depths and experiences a new dimension of unity. The other area of relationship concerns the people who profess non-Christian religions or live without religion, and the proclamation to them of the Jesus of whom Peter said to the Pharisees: "There is salvation in no one else, for there is no other name under heaven given among mortals by which we must be saved" (Acts 4:12). The pope explains the relationship between dialogue and proclamation in this document. He shows that mission, the proclamation of Christ to all those who do not know him, remains a permanent obligation because every person is waiting for the One in whom God and man are one, he who is the "Redeemer of man."

The encyclicals on man

Finally we come to the three great encyclicals in which the anthropological theme is developed under various aspects. *Veritatis Splendor* does not aim only at the crisis in moral theology within the Church, but belongs to the worldwide debate over ethos, which today has become a question of life and death for humanity. In the decades before the [Second Vatican] Council, there was already a decisive movement opposing a form of moral theology that, in the nineteenth century, had become ever more preoccupyingly reduced to casuistry. Christian moral doctrine had to be reconsidered in its great positive perspective, beginning from the heart of the faith, and not considered a list of prohibitions. The idea of the imitation of Christ and the principle of love were developed as fundamental guiding ideas, from which individual doctrines could emerge organically. The willingness to be inspired by the faith as by a new light that renders moral doctrine transparent led to a departure from the version of morality based on natural law in favor of one patterned on the Bible and salvation history. The Second Vatican Council con-

firmed and restated these approaches, but the attempt
to construct a purely biblical form of morality
became impractical in the face of the concrete questions of our time. Pure biblicism is not a possible
approach in moral theology. So the brief phase that
attempted to give moral theology a biblical inspiration was followed, with surprising rapidity, by the
attempt to provide a purely rational form of ethos.
But the return to the concept of the doctrine of natural law was blocked: the antimetaphysical current
that may have had a role in the attempt at biblicism
made natural law seem like an antiquated, outdated
model. One thus remained at the mercy of a posi-
tivistic form of reasoning that no longer recognized
the good as such. As one moral theologian at the time
put it: "The good is always only that which is better
than...." Calculation of the consequences remained
the criterion—the moral [action] is that which seems
the most positive, considering the foreseeable consequences. Consequentialism was not always applied in
such a radical way, but ultimately what resulted was a
system that sets aside what is moral because the good
as such does not exist. For such a form of reasoning,
not even the Bible has anything to say. It can provide
motivation, but not content. But if that's the way
things are, Christianity as a "way"—as it should and
wants to be—is finished. And if at first orthopraxis
was used as a refuge from orthodoxy, it now has

become a tragic irony—because, at its foundation, it does not exist.

The pope has, to the contrary, given decisive legitimacy to the metaphysical perspective—which is simply a consequence of trust in creation. Once again, beginning from trust in creation, he succeeds in connecting and blending anthropocentrism and geocentrism: "...reason draws its own truth and authority from the eternal law, which is none other than divine wisdom itself...the natural law 'is nothing other than the light of understanding infused in us by God.'"[22] It is precisely because the pope sides with metaphysics, through his trust in creation, that he can also understand the Bible as a Word spoken now, that he can connect the metaphysical and biblical construction of the theos. One pearl of the encyclical, both philosophically and theologically meaningful, is the great passage on martyrdom. If there is nothing left worth dying for, then life itself becomes empty. It is only if there is absolute good worth dying for, and eternal evil can never become good, that we are confirmed in our dignity and protected from the dictatorship of ideologies.

The dignity of all human life

This point is also fundamental for the encyclical *Evangelium Vitae,* which the pope wrote at the pressing invitation of bishops worldwide, but it is also an expression of his impassioned struggle for the absolute respect of the dignity of human life. Wherever human life is treated as a mere biological reality, it becomes the object of the calculation of consequences. But the pope, together with the Church's faith, sees in man, in every man—little or great, weak or strong, as useful or useless as he may appear—the image of God; Christ, the Son of God himself made man, died for every man. This confers infinite value and absolutely inviolable dignity upon every individual. Because in man there is more than mere *bios,* his biological life also becomes infinitely valuable. It is not at anyone's disposal, because it is vested with dignity by God. There are no consequences, no matter how noble they may seem, that can justify experiments on man. After all the cruel experiences of the abuse of man, as highly moral as their motivations might have appeared, this was and is a necessary message. It becomes clear that the faith is humanity's refuge.

In the situation of the metaphysical ignorance in which we find ourselves, and which becomes at the same time moral atrophy, faith presents itself as man's ability to save himself. The pope, as a spokesman for the faith, defends man against an apparent morality that threatens to crush him.

The courage of reason

Finally, we must consider the great encyclical *Fides et Ratio,* on faith and reason. The theme of the truth, which characterizes all of the Holy Father's magisterial work, is developed here in all of its drama. Asserting the idea that the truth is knowable, or proclaiming the Christian message as an acknowledged truth, is viewed to a large extent today as an attack against tolerance and pluralism. "Truth" even becomes a forbidden word. But it is precisely here that the dignity of man enters into play once again. If man is not capable of finding the truth, then everything that he thinks and does is pure conventionalism, mere "tradition." Nothing remains for him—as we have already seen—but the calculation of consequences. But who can truly comprehend the consequences of human actions? If this is the way things are, then all the religions are mere traditions, and, naturally, even the proclamation of the faith is a colonialistic or imperialistic pretense. This proclamation is not in contradiction to human dignity only when the faith is true, because the truth harms no one; on the contrary, it is the good that we owe to each other. Following the great successes in the natural sciences and technology, reason has lost courage in the face of man's great questions about God, death, eternity, and the moral life. Positivism spreads over man's interior eye like a cataract. But if these questions, ultimately decisive for our lives, are relegated to the realm of pure subjectivity and arbitrariness, then we have become blind to what pertains to being human. Beginning with the faith, the pope asks that reason have the courage to recognize fundamental realities. If the faith does not stand in the light of reason, it plunges into mere tradition and thus declares its profound arbitrariness. Faith needs the courage of reason. Reason is not contrary to faith, but urges it to demand from itself the great things for which it was created. *Sapere aude!*[23] Demand great things of yourself! You are destined for this. The faith, says the pope, does not want to silence reason, but wants to free it from the veil that obscures from it humanity's great questions. Once again one sees that the faith defends man in his human existence. Joseph Pieper once expressed the thought that "in the final epoch of history, beneath the dominion of the sophist and of a corrupt pseudophilosophy, true philosophy will be able to restore its primordial unity with theology," and that therefore, at the end of history, "the root of everything and the ultimate meaning of existence—the specific object of the exercise of philosophy—will be considered only by those who believe."

We are now—as far as we can know—at the end of history. But we run the risk of withholding from reason its true greatness. And the pope rightly considers it the task of faith to urge reason once again to have the courage to face the truth. Without reason, faith crumbles to ruins; without faith, reason risks atrophying. What is at stake is man. But in order that man might be redeemed, there is need for the Redeemer; we need the man Christ, who is both man and God "in an unconfused and undivided way" in a single person, *Redemptor hominis*.[24]

CHAPTER III

The Poetry of John Paul II

Roman Triptych: Meditations
Thursday, March 6, 2003

First Panel: The majesty of creation

The first panel of Pope John Paul II's *Roman Triptych* mirrors the experience of creation, its beauty and its life. In it appears the image of the wooded hills and the even more vivid image of the waters rushing toward the valley, the "silvery cascade, rhythmically falling from the mountain." In this connection several sentences came to mind that were written by Karol Wojtyla in 1976, when he preached the retreat for Paul VI and the Curia. He related the case of a physicist with whom he had carried on a long discussion, and at the end of which he had said to him: "From the point of view of my science and its method, I'm an atheist...." However, in a letter, the same man wrote: "Every time I find myself before the majesty of nature, of the mountains, I feel that HE exists." One can speak of two different ways of perceiving nature! Certainly, the first panel of the *Triptych* closes almost timidly on the threshold. The pope does not yet speak directly of God, but he prays, as one prays to a still unknown God. "Allow me to wet my lips in spring water, to feel its freshness, reviving freshness." With these words he seeks its source and receives direction: "If you want to find the source, you have to go up, against the current." In the first verse of his meditation, he said: "The undulating wood slopes down"; woods and waters have shown a downward movement. His pursuit of the source, however, now obliges him to climb up, to move against the tide.

Next panels: The end and the beginning, the vision of God

I consider that this is the key to the interpretation of the two following panels. Indeed, they guide us in the climb upward "against the current." The spiritual pilgrimage, accomplished in this text, leads toward the "Beginning." On arriving, the true surprise is that the "beginning" also reveals the "end." Whoever knows the origin also sees the "where" and "why" of the entire movement of "being," which is becoming, and, exactly in this way, also enduring: "Everything endures, continually becoming." The name of the source that the pilgrim discovers is, above all, the "Word," according to the first words of the Bible: "God said," and which John took up and reformulated in an unmatched way in his Gospel: "In the beginning was the Word." However, the true key word that sums up the pilgrimage in the second panel of the *Triptych* is not "Word," but rather vision and seeing. The Word has a face. The Word—the source—is a vision. Creation, the universe, proceeds from a vision. And the human person comes from a vision. This key word, therefore, leads the pope while he meditates on Michelangelo's frescoes in the Sistine Chapel, which have become so dear to him. In the images of the world, Michelangelo discerned the vision of God. He saw with the creative gaze of God, and, through this gaze, he reproduced on walls, by means of daring frescoes, the original vision from which all reality derives. In Michelangelo, who helps us to rediscover the vision of God in the world's images, there seems to be realized, in an exemplary way, what all of us are destined to enjoy. The pope says of Adam and Eve, who represent the human being in general, men and women: "So they too became sharers of that gaze...." Every human person is called to "recover that gaze again." The way to the source is a path that leads us to become seeing, to learn from God how to see. Then the beginning and the end appear. Then the human person becomes just.

Epilogue to the Second Panel:
Last Judgment, conclaves

The link between the beginning and the end—for the pope, probably, a pilgrim journeying inward and upward—appeared obvious in the Sistine Chapel, where Michelangelo presents to us the images of the beginning and the end, the vision of creation and the impressive depiction of the Last Judgment. The contemplation of the Last Judgment in the epilogue of the second panel is perhaps the part of the *Triptych* that most moves the reader. From the pope's interior eye emerges, in a fresh way, the memory of the conclaves of August and October 1978. Since I was also present, I know well how we were exposed to those images in the hour of the important decisions, how they challenged us, and how they instilled in our souls the greatness of our responsibility. The pope speaks to the cardinals of the future conclave, "after my death," and says that Michelangelo's vision will speak to them. The word "con-clave"[25] makes one think of the keys, of the patrimony of the keys handed to Peter. To place these keys in the right hands:

this is the immense responsibility of those days. Here we recall the words of Jesus to the lawyers, "Woe to you lawyers! For you have taken away the key of knowledge" (Lk 11:52). Michelangelo urges us not to take away the key, but to use it to open the door so that everyone may enter.

Second Panel: Creation—dialogue in God

However, let us return to the true center of the second panel, a look at the "origins." What do people see there? In Michelangelo's work, the Creator appears "in the likeness of a human being": the image and likeness of the human person with God is contrasted in such a way that we can deduce the humanity of God, which makes it possible to represent the Creator. However, the view that Christ has opened for us directs our gaze far beyond this and, by contrast, starting with the Creator, with the beginnings, shows who the human person really is. The Creator —the beginning—is not, as might appear in Michelangelo's painting, simply the "Almighty Ancient One." Instead, he is "a communion of persons, a mutual exchange...." If, at first, we saw God beginning from man, we now learn to see the human person beginning from God: a reciprocal gift of self—the human person is destined for this. If he manages to find the way to achieve this, he is a mirror of God's essence, and so reveals the link between the beginning and the end.

Third Panel: Abraham and Isaac's ascent of Mount Moria, total self-giving

The immense arch, the true vision of the *Roman Triptych*, is clearly revealed in the third panel: the ascent by Abraham and Isaac of Mount Moria, the mountain of sacrifice, of self-gift without reservation. This ascent is the last and decisive stage in Abraham's journey, which began with his departure from his own land, Ur of the Chaldeans; it is the basic stage of the ascent toward the summit, against the current, to the source that is also the goal. In the inexhaustible dialogue between father and son—consisting of few words and bearing together in silence the mystery of these words—all the questions of history, the suffering, fears, and hopes are reflected. In the end, it becomes clear that this dialogue between father and son, between Abraham and Isaac, is a dialogue within God himself, the dialogue between the eternal Father and his Son, the Word, and that this eternal dialogue represents at the same time the response to our unfinished human dialogue. Indeed, in the end Isaac is saved—the lamb is a mysterious sign of the Son, who becomes the Lamb and a sacrificial victim, thus revealing to us the true face of

God: the God who gives himself to us, who is entirely gift and love, to the very end (cf. Jn 13:1). Thus, in this very concrete event of history, which seems to take us so far from the great visions of creation in the first panel of the *Triptych,* there appears clearly the beginning and the end of all things, the link between the descent and ascent, between the source, the way, and the end of the journey: we recognize God who gives himself, who is simultaneously the beginning, the way, and the final goal. This God appears in creation and in history. He seeks us in our sufferings and in our questioning. He shows us what it means to be human persons: to give ourselves in love, which makes us like God. Through the journey of the Son to the mountain of sacrifice, there is revealed "the mystery hidden from the foundations of the world." The love that gives is the original mystery, and in loving, we too can understand the message of creation and find the way.

Chapter IV

Homily for the Funeral Mass

Our Beloved Pope Now Stands
at the Window of the Father's House
Friday, April 8, 2005

"Follow me!" The Risen Lord says these words to Peter. They are his last words to this disciple, chosen to shepherd his flock. "Follow me"—this lapidary saying of Christ can be taken as the key to understanding the message that comes to us from the life of our late beloved Pope John Paul II. Today we bury his remains in the earth as a seed of immortality—our hearts are full of sadness, yet at the same time of joyful hope and profound gratitude.

These are the sentiments that inspire us, brothers and sisters in Christ, present here in Saint Peter's

Square, in neighboring streets, and in various other locations within the city of Rome, where an immense crowd, silently praying, has gathered over the last few days. I greet all of you from my heart. In the name of the College of Cardinals, I also wish to express my respects to heads of state, heads of government, and the delegations from various countries. I greet the authorities and official representatives of other Churches and Christian communities, and likewise those of different religions. Next I greet the archbishops, bishops, priests, religious men and women, and the faithful who have come here from every continent, especially the young, whom John Paul II liked to call the future and the hope of the Church. My greeting is extended, moreover, to all those throughout the world who are united with us through radio and television in this solemn celebration of our beloved Holy Father's funeral.

John Paul II's priestly vocation

"Follow me!" As a young student, Karol Wojtyla was thrilled by literature, the theater, and poetry. Working in a chemical plant, surrounded and threatened by the Nazi terror, he heard the voice of the Lord: Follow me! In this extraordinary setting, he began to read books of philosophy and theology, and then entered the clandestine seminary established by

Cardinal Sapieha. After the war, he was able to complete his studies in the faculty of theology of the Jagiellonian University of Kraków. How often, in his letters to priests and in his autobiographical books, has he spoken to us about his priesthood, to which he was ordained on November 1, 1946. In these texts he interprets his priesthood with particular reference to three sayings of the Lord. First: "You did not choose me, but I chose you. And I appointed you to go and bear fruit, fruit that will last" (Jn 15:16). The second saying is: "The good shepherd lays down his life for the sheep" (Jn 10:11). And then: "As the Father has loved me, so I have loved you; abide in my love" (Jn 15:9). In these three sayings we see the heart and soul of our Holy Father. He really went everywhere, untiringly, in order to bear fruit, fruit that lasts. *Rise, Let Us Be on Our Way!* is the title of his next-to-last book. "Rise, let us be on our way!"—with these words he roused us from a lethargic faith, from the sleep of the disciples of both yesterday and today. "Rise, let us be on our way!" he continues to say to us even today. The Holy Father was a priest to the last, for he offered his life to God for his flock and for the entire human family, in a daily self-oblation for the service of the Church, especially amid the sufferings of his final months. And in this way he became one with Christ, the Good Shepherd who loves his sheep. Finally, "abide in my love": the pope who tried to meet everyone, who had an ability to forgive and to open his heart to all, tells us once again today, with these words of the Lord, that by abiding in the love of Christ, we learn, at the school of Christ, the art of true love.

Bishop of Kraków

"Follow me!" In July 1958, the young priest Karol Wojtyla began a new stage in his journey with the Lord and in the footsteps of the Lord. Karol had gone to the Masuri lakes for his usual vacation, along with a group of young people who loved canoeing. But he brought with him a letter inviting him to call on the Primate of Poland, Cardinal Wyszynski. He could guess the purpose of the meeting: he was to be appointed as the auxiliary Bishop of Kraków. Leaving the academic world, leaving this challenging engagement with young people, leaving the great intellectual endeavor of striving to understand and interpret the mystery of that creature which is man and of communicating to today's world the Christian interpretation of our being—all this must have seemed to him like losing his very self, losing what had become the very human identity of this young priest. "Follow me!" Karol Wojtyla accepted the appointment, for he heard in the Church's call the voice of Christ. And then he realized how true are the Lord's words: "Those who try to make their life secure will lose it, but those who lose their life will keep it" (Lk 17:33). Our pope—and we all know this—never wanted to make his own life secure, to keep it for himself; he wanted to give of himself unreservedly, to the very last moment, for Christ, and thus also for us. And thus he came to experience how everything that he had given over into the Lord's hands came back to him in a new way. His love of words, of poetry, of literature, became an essential part of his pastoral mission and gave new vitality, new urgency, new attractiveness to the preaching of the Gospel, even when it was a sign of contradiction.

The shepherd of Christ's flock

"Follow me!" In October 1978, Cardinal Wojtyla once again heard the voice of the Lord. Once more there took place that dialogue with Peter reported in the Gospel of this Mass: "Simon, son of John, do you love me? Feed my sheep!" [Jn 21:16]. To the Lord's question, "Karol, do you love me?" the Archbishop of Kraków answered from the depths of his heart: "Lord you know everything; you know that I love you." The love of Christ was the dominant force in the life of our beloved Holy Father. Anyone who ever saw him pray, who ever heard him preach, knows that. Thanks to his being profoundly rooted in Christ, he was able to bear a burden that transcends merely human abilities: that of being the shepherd of Christ's flock, his universal Church. This is not the time to speak of the specific content of this rich pontificate. I would like only to read two passages of today's liturgy that reflect central elements of his message. In the first reading, Saint Peter says—and with Saint Peter, the pope himself—"I truly understand that God shows no partiality, but in every nation anyone who fears him and does what is right is acceptable to him. You know the message he sent to the people of Israel, preaching peace by Jesus Christ—he is Lord of all" (Acts 10:34–36). And in the second reading, Saint Paul—and with Saint Paul, our late pope—exhorts us, crying out: "My brothers and sisters, whom I love and long for, my joy and my crown, stand firm in the Lord in this way, my beloved" (Phil 4:1).

John Paul II interpreted
the paschal mystery for us

"Follow me!" Together with the command to feed his flock, Christ proclaimed to Peter that he would die a martyr's death. With those words, which conclude and sum up the dialogue on love and on the mandate of the universal shepherd, the Lord recalls another dialogue, which took place during the Last Supper. There Jesus had said: "Where I am going, you cannot come." Peter said to him, "Lord, where are you going?" Jesus replied: "Where I am going, you cannot follow me now; but you will follow me afterward" (Jn 13:33, 36). From the supper, Jesus went toward the cross, toward his resurrection—he entered into the paschal mystery; and Peter could not yet follow him. Now—after the resurrection—comes the time, comes this "afterward." By shepherding the flock of Christ, Peter enters into the paschal mystery, he goes toward the cross and the resurrection. The Lord says this in these words: "...when you were younger, you used to fasten your own belt and to go wherever you wished. But when you grow old, you will stretch out your hands, and someone else will fasten a belt around you and take you where you do not wish to go" (Jn 21:18). In the first years of his pontificate, still young and full of energy, the Holy Father went to the very ends of the earth, guided by Christ. But afterward, he increasingly entered into the communion of Christ's sufferings; increasingly he understood the truth of the words: "Someone else will fasten a belt around you." And in this very communion with the suffering Lord, tirelessly and with renewed intensity, he proclaimed the Gospel, the mystery of that love which goes to the end (cf. Jn 13:1).

He interpreted for us the paschal mystery as a mystery of divine mercy. In his last book, he wrote that the limit imposed upon evil "is ultimately Divine Mercy."[26] And reflecting on the assassination attempt [on his life], he said:

> In sacrificing himself for us all, Christ gave a new meaning to suffering, opening up a new dimension, a new order: the order of love.... It is this suffering which burns and consumes evil with the flame of love and draws forth even from sin a great flowering of good.[27]

Impelled by this vision, the pope suffered and loved in communion with Christ, and that is why the message of his suffering and his silence proved so eloquent and so fruitful.

Divine Mercy: the Holy Father found the purest reflection of God's mercy in the Mother of God. He, who at an early age had lost his own mother, loved his heavenly Mother all the more. He heard the words of the crucified Lord as addressed personally to him: "Behold your Mother," and so he did as the beloved disciple did: "he took her into his own home" (*eis ta idia*[28]: Jn 19:27)—*Totus tuus.* And from the Mother, he learned to conform himself to Christ.

None of us can ever forget how on that last Easter Sunday of his life, the Holy Father, marked by suffering, came once more to the window of the Apostolic Palace and one last time gave his blessing *Urbi et Orbi.*[29] We can be sure that our beloved pope is standing today at the window of the Father's house, that he sees us and blesses us. Yes, bless us, Holy Father. We entrust your dear soul to the Mother of God, your Mother, who guided you each day and who will guide you now to the eternal glory of her Son, our Lord Jesus Christ. Amen.

PART II

BENEDICT XVI
ON
POPE JOHN PAUL II

2006

Chapter V

"Let Yourselves Be Surprised by Christ!"

Apostolic Journey to Cologne on the Occasion of the Twentieth World Youth Day

Cologne, August 18, 2006

To the Young People Waiting for the Pope Along the Banks of the Rhine

Dear young people, I am delighted to meet you here in Cologne on the banks of the Rhine! You have come from various parts of Germany, Europe, and the rest of the world as pilgrims in the footsteps of the Magi. Following their route, you too want to find Jesus. Like them, you have begun this journey in order to contemplate, both personally and with others, the face of God revealed by the Child in the manger. Like yourselves, I too have set out to join you in kneeling before the consecrated white host in which the eyes of faith recognize the Real Presence of the Savior of the world. Together, we will continue to meditate on the theme of this World Youth Day: *"We have come to worship him"* (Mt 2:2).

The memory of John Paul II

With great joy I welcome you, dear young people. You have come here from near and far, walking the streets of the world and the pathways of life. My particular greeting goes to those who, like the Magi, have come from the East. You are the representatives of so many of our brothers and sisters who are waiting, without realizing it, for the star to rise in their skies and lead them to Christ, Light of the Nations, in whom they will find the fullest response to their hearts' deepest desires. I also greet with affection those among you who have not been baptized, and those of you who do not yet know Christ or have not yet found a home in his Church. Pope John Paul II had invited you in particular to come to this gathering; I thank you for deciding to come to Cologne. Some of you might perhaps describe your adolescence in the words with which Edith Stein, who later lived in the Carmel in Cologne, described her own: "I consciously and deliberately lost the habit of praying." During these days, you can once again have a moving experience of prayer as dialogue with God, the God whom we know loves us and whom we in turn wish to love. To all of you I appeal: Open wide your hearts to God! Let yourselves be surprised by Christ! Let him have "the right of free speech" during these days! Open the doors of your freedom to his merciful love! Share your joys and pains with Christ, and let him enlighten your minds with his light and touch your hearts with his grace. In these days blessed with sharing and joy, may you have a liberating experience of the Church as the place where God's merciful love reaches out to all people. In the Church and through the Church you will meet Christ, who is waiting for you.

Today, as I arrived in Cologne to take part with you in the twentieth World Youth Day, I naturally recall with deep gratitude the Servant of God so greatly loved by us all, Pope John Paul II, who had the inspired idea of calling young people from all over the world to join in celebrating Christ, the one Redeemer of the human race. Thanks to the profound dialogue that developed over more than twenty years between the pope and young people, many of them were able to deepen their faith, forge bonds of communion, and develop a love for the Good News of salvation in Christ and a desire to proclaim it throughout the world. That great pope understood the challenges faced by young people today, and, as a sign of his trust in them, he did not hesitate to spur them on to be courageous heralds of the Gospel and intrepid builders of the civilization of truth, love, and peace.

Pilgrims in the footsteps of the Magi

Today it is my turn to take up this extraordinary spiritual legacy bequeathed to us by Pope John Paul II. He loved you—you realized that and you returned his love with all your youthful enthusiasm. Now all of us together have to put his teaching into practice. It is this commitment that has brought us here to Cologne, as pilgrims in the footsteps of the Magi. According to tradition, the names of the Magi in Greek were Melchior, Gaspar, and Balthasar. Matthew, in his Gospel, tells of the question that burned in the hearts of the Magi: "Where is the infant king of the Jews?" (Mt 2:2). It was in order to search for him that they set out on the long journey to Jerusalem. This was why they withstood hardships and sacrifices, and never yielded to discouragement or the temptation to give up and go home. Now that they were close to their goal, they had no other question than this. We, too, have come to Cologne because in our hearts we have the same urgent question that prompted the Magi from the East to set out on their journey, even if it is differently expressed. It is true that today we are no longer looking for a king, but we are concerned for the state of the world and we are asking: "Where do I find standards to live by? What are the criteria that govern responsible cooperation in building the present and the future of our world? On whom can I rely? To whom shall I entrust myself? Where is the One who can offer me the response capable of satisfying my heart's deepest desires?" The fact that we ask questions like these means that we realize our journey is not over until we meet the One who has the power to establish that universal kingdom of justice and peace to which all people aspire, but which they are unable to build by themselves. Asking such questions also means searching for Someone who can neither deceive nor be deceived, and who therefore can offer a certainty so solid that we can live for it and, if need be, even die for it.

Dear friends, when questions like these appear on the horizon of life, we must be able to make the necessary choices. It is like finding ourselves at a cross-

roads: which direction do we take? The one prompted by the passions or the one indicated by the star
that shines in your conscience? The Magi heard the
answer: "In Bethlehem of Judea; for so it is written by
the prophet" (Mt 2:5), and, enlightened by these
words, they chose to press forward to the very end.
From Jerusalem they went on to Bethlehem. In other
words, they went from the word that showed them
where to find the King of the Jews whom they were
seeking, all the way to the end, to an encounter with
the King who was at the same time the Lamb of God
who takes away the sins of the world. Those words
are also spoken for us. We also have a choice to make.
If we think about it, this is precisely our experience
when we share in the Eucharist. For in every Mass the
Liturgy of the Word introduces us to our participation in the mystery of the cross and resurrection of
Christ and, hence, introduces us to the Eucharistic
Meal, to union with Christ. Present on the altar is the
One whom the Magi saw lying in the manger: Christ,
the living Bread who came down from heaven to give
life to the world, the true Lamb who gives his own life
for the salvation of humanity. Enlightened by the
Word, it is in Bethlehem—the "House of Bread"—
that we can always encounter the inconceivable
greatness of a God who humbled himself even to
appearing in a manger, to giving himself as food on
the altar.

Happiness has the face of Jesus

We can imagine the awe the Magi experienced before the Child in swaddling clothes. Only faith enabled them to recognize in the face of that Child the King whom they were seeking, the God to whom the star had guided them. In him, crossing the abyss between the finite and the infinite, the visible and the invisible, the Eternal entered time, the Mystery became known by entrusting himself to us in the frail body of a small child. "The Magi are filled with awe by what they see; heaven on earth and earth in heaven; man in God and God in man; they see enclosed in a tiny body the One whom the entire world cannot contain."[30] In these days, during this "Year of the Eucharist," we will turn with the same awe to Christ present in the Tabernacle of Mercy, in the Sacrament of the Altar.

Dear young people, the happiness you are seeking, the happiness you have a right to enjoy has a name and a face: it is Jesus of Nazareth, hidden in the Eucharist. Only he gives the fullness of life to humanity! With Mary, say your own "yes" to God, for he wishes to give himself to you. I repeat today what I said at the beginning of my pontificate: "If we let Christ into our lives, we lose nothing, nothing, absolutely nothing of what makes life free, beautiful, and great. No! Only in this friendship are the doors of life opened wide. Only in this friendship is the great potential of human existence truly revealed. Only in this friendship do we experience beauty and liberation."[31] Be completely convinced of this: Christ takes from you nothing that is beautiful and great, but brings everything to perfection for the glory of God, the happiness of men and women, and the salvation of the world.

In these days I encourage you to commit yourselves without reserve to serving Christ, whatever the cost. The encounter with Jesus Christ will allow you to experience in your hearts the joy of his living and life-giving presence and enable you to bear witness to it before others. Let your presence in this city be the first sign and proclamation of the Gospel, thanks to the witness of your actions and your joy. Let us raise our hearts in a hymn of praise and thanksgiving to the Father for the many blessings he has given us and for the gift of faith that we will celebrate together, making it manifest to the world from this land in the heart of Europe, a Europe that owes so much to the Gospel and its witnesses down the centuries.

And now I shall go as a pilgrim to the Cathedral of Cologne, to venerate the relics of the holy Magi who left everything to follow the star that was guiding them to the Savior of the human race. You too, dear young people, have already had, or will have, the opportunity to make the same pilgrimage. These relics are only the poor and frail sign of what those men were and what they experienced so many centuries ago. The relics direct us toward God himself: it is he who, by the power of his grace, grants to weak human beings the courage to bear witness to him before the world. By inviting us to venerate the mortal remains of the martyrs and saints, the Church does not forget that, in the end, these are indeed just human bones, but they are bones that belonged to individuals touched by the living power of God. The relics of the saints are traces of that invisible but real presence that sheds light upon the shadows of the world and reveals the kingdom of heaven in our midst. They cry out with us and for us: "Maranatha!"—"Come, Lord Jesus!" My dear friends, I make these words my farewell, and I invite you to the Saturday evening vigil. I shall see you then!

The 1980 Synod of Bishops in the Vatican. Standing with John Paul II, to the left: Cardinal Gantin, Cardinal Picachy, Cardinal Primatesta; to the right: Monsignor Tomko, Cardinal Ratzinger.

Pope John Paul II signing the new Roman Catholic Code of Canon Law, *while Cardinal Joseph Ratzinger looks over the his shoulder (January 25, 1983).*

John Paul II and Cardinal Joseph Ratzinger during the 1990 Synod of Bishops.

Pope John Paul II greets Cardinal Joseph Ratzinger during a meeting with cardinals and bishops in the Paul VI Hall at the Vatican on October 18, 2003.

Cardinal Joseph Ratzinger incenses the coffin of the late Pope John Paul II at the end of the funeral Mass at Saint Peter's Square in the Vatican, April 8, 2005.

On the first anniversary of the death of Pope John Paul II, Pope Benedict XVI visits his tomb, located in the grotto beneath Saint Peter's Basilica at the Vatican (April 6, 2006).

Benedict XVI, during the meeting with the populace in Rynek Plaza in Warsaw, displaying an image of his predecessor, Pope John Paul II.

Pope Benedict XVI at the window of his private apartment at the Vatican reciting the Rosary on the first anniversary of the death of Pope John Paul II, April 2, 2006.

Chapter VI

Our Beloved Pope John Paul II

On the First Anniversary of His Death

Angelus Message
(April 2, 2006)

Dear brothers and sisters, on April 2 last year, just as today, in these very hours and here in this very apartment, beloved Pope John Paul II was living the last stage of his earthly pilgrimage, a pilgrimage of faith, love, and hope, which left a profound mark on the history of the Church and of humanity. His agony and death constitute, as it were, an extension of the Easter Triduum. We all remember the images of his last Way of the Cross on Good Friday: being unable to go to the Colosseum, he followed it in his private chapel, a cross in his hands. Then, on Easter morning he imparted the *Urbi et Orbi* blessing, unable to speak, solely with the gesture of his hand. Let us never forget that blessing. It was the most heartfelt and moving blessing that he left us as the last testimony of his desire to carry out his ministry to the very end. John Paul II died as he had always lived, inspired by the indomitable courage of faith, abandoning himself to God, and entrusting himself to Mary Most Holy. This evening we will commemorate him with a Marian prayer vigil in Saint Peter's Square, where tomorrow afternoon we will celebrate Mass for him.

A year after his departure from this earth to the Father's house, we can ask ourselves: What did this great pope who led the Church into the third millennium leave us? His legacy is immense, but the message of his very long pontificate can be summed up well in the words [with which] he chose to inaugurate it, here in Saint Peter's Square on October 22, 1978: "Open wide the doors to Christ!"[32] John Paul II incarnated this unforgettable appeal, which I feel resounding within me as if it were yesterday, in the whole of himself and in the whole of his mission as Successor of Peter, especially with his extraordinary program of apostolic journeys. In visiting the countries of the entire world, meeting the crowds, the ecclesial communities, the heads of governments, religious leaders, and various social realities, he was making, as it were, a great gesture to confirm his initial words. He always proclaimed Christ, presenting him to everyone, as did the Second Vatican Council, as an answer to man's expectations, expectations of freedom, justice, and peace. Christ is the Redeemer of man, he was fond of repeating, the one genuine Savior of every person and the entire human race.

In his last years, the Lord gradually stripped him of everything to make him fully resemble him. And when, henceforth, he could no longer travel or even walk, or finally even speak, his gesture, his proclamation, was reduced to the essential: the gift of himself to the very end. His death was the fulfillment of a consistent witness of faith that moved the hearts of so many people of good will. John Paul II departed from us on a Saturday dedicated especially to Mary, for whom he had always had a filial devotion. Let us now ask the heavenly Mother of God to help us treasure what this great pope gave and taught us.

༺ঞ༻

Words to Those Gathered
for the Holy Rosary

(April 2, 2006)

Dear brothers and sisters, we are meeting this evening, on the first anniversary of the departure of beloved Pope John Paul II, for this Marian vigil organized by the Diocese of Rome. I greet with affection all of you present here in Saint Peter's Square, starting with the Cardinal Vicar Camillo Ruini and the auxiliary bishops, with a special thought for the cardinals, bishops, priests, and religious, and for the lay faithful, especially the youth. Truly, the entire city of Rome is symbolically gathered for this emotional moment of prayer and reflection. I address a special greeting to Cardinal Stanislaw Dziwisz, Metropolitan Archbishop of Kraków, who is linked to us by television, and who was for many years a faithful collaborator of the late pontiff. A year has already passed since the death of the Servant of God John Paul II at this very moment—it was 9:37 P.M.—but his memory lives on, more alive than ever, as is testified to by the many events scheduled to take place in these days throughout the world. He continues to be present in our minds and hearts; he continues to communicate to us his love for God and his love for man; he continues to inspire in one and all, and especially in the young, enthusiasm for good and the courage to follow Jesus and his teachings.

How can we sum up the life and evangelical witness of this great pontiff? I will attempt to do so by using two words: "fidelity" and "dedication"—total fidelity to God and unreserved dedication to his mission as pastor of the universal Church. Fidelity and dedication appeared even more convincing and moving in his final months, when he embodied in himself what he wrote in 1984 in the Apostolic Letter *Salvifici Doloris*: "Suffering is present in the world in order to release love, in order to give birth to works of love toward our neighbor, in order to transform the whole of human civilization into a 'civilization of love.'"[33] His courageously-faced illness made everyone more attentive to human suffering, to all physical and spiritual pain; he gave dignity and value to suffering, witnessing that the human being's value does not depend on his efficiency or appearance but on himself, because he was created and loved by God. With his words and gestures, the dear John Paul II never tired of pointing out to the world that if a person allows himself to be embraced by Christ, he does not repress the riches of his humanity; if he adheres to Christ with all his heart, he will never lack anything. On the contrary, the encounter with Christ makes our lives more impassioned. Precisely because he drew ever closer to God in prayer, contemplation, and love for Truth and Beauty, our beloved pope was able to become the traveling companion of each one of us and even to speak authoritatively to those who had nothing to do with the Christian faith.

This evening, the first anniversary of his return to the Father's house, we are invited to accept anew the spiritual legacy he has bequeathed to us; we are urged, among other things, to live by seeking tirelessly the Truth that alone brings relief to our hearts. We are encouraged not to be afraid to follow Christ in order to bring everyone the Gospel proclamation that is the leaven of a more fraternal and supportive humanity. May John Paul II help us from heaven to continue on our way, remaining docile disciples of Jesus in order to be, as he himself loved to repeat to young people, "dawn watchmen" at the beginning of this third Christian millennium. For this, let us call on Mary, Mother of the Redeemer, for whom he always felt a tender devotion.

ᵒᵍ⚜ᵍᵒ

Homily at the Mass for John Paul II:
His Sincere and Solid Faith

(April 3, 2006)

Dear brothers and sisters, in these days, on the first anniversary of his death, the memory of the Servant of God John Paul II is particularly vivid throughout the Church and the world. With the Marian vigil yesterday evening, we relived the precise moment of his devout passing one year ago, whereas today we are here in this same Saint Peter's Square to offer the Eucharistic Sacrifice in suffrage for his chosen soul. Together with the cardinals, bishops, priests, and religious, I greet with affection the numerous pilgrims who have arrived from very many places, especially from Poland, to bear witness to their esteem, affection, and deep gratitude. Let us pray for this beloved pontiff, allowing ourselves to be illuminated by the Word of God we have just heard.

In the first reading from the Book of Wisdom, we were reminded of the eternal destiny that awaits the righteous: a destiny of superabundant happiness, an incomparable reward for the sufferings and trials they faced during their lives. "God tested them and found them worthy of himself; like gold in the furnace he tried them, and like a sacrificial burnt offering he

accepted them" (Wis 3:5–6). The term "burnt offering" refers to the sacrifice in which the victim was
entirely burned, consumed by the flames; consequently, it was a sign of total offering to God. This
biblical expression reminds us of the mission of John
Paul II, who made his life a gift to God and to the
Church and, especially in the celebration of the
Eucharist, lived out the sacrificial dimension of his
priesthood. Among the invocations dear to him was
one that comes from the "Litany of our Lord Jesus
Christ, Priest and Victim" that he chose to place at
the end of his book, *Gift and Mystery,* published on the
occasion of the fiftieth anniversary of his ordination
to the priesthood: "*Iesu, Pontifex qui tradidisti temetip-
sum Deo oblationem et hostiam*—Jesus, High Priest who
gave yourself to God as offering and victim, have
mercy on us."[34] How frequently he repeated this
invocation! It expresses clearly the profoundly priestly character of his whole life. He never made a mystery of his desire to become increasingly one with
Christ the Priest through the Eucharistic Sacrifice, a
source of tireless apostolic dedication.

It was faith, of course, that was at the root of this
total offering of himself. In the second reading that
we have just heard, Saint Peter too uses the image of
gold tested by fire and applies it to faith (cf. 1 Pt 1:7).
In fact, in life's difficulties it is especially the quality
of the faith of each one of us that is tried and test-

ed: its firmness, its purity, its consistency with life.
The late pontiff, whom God had endowed with mul-
tiple human and spiritual gifts, in passing through the
crucible of apostolic labors and sickness, appeared
more and more as a "rock" of faith. To those who had
the opportunity to be close to him, that firm and
forthright faith was almost tangible. If it impressed
the circle of his collaborators, it did not fail during
his long pontificate to spread its beneficial influence
throughout the Church in a crescendo that reached
its highest point in the last months and days of his
life. It was a convinced, strong, and authentic faith—
free of the fears and compromises that have infected
the hearts of so many people, thanks partly to his
many apostolic pilgrimages in every part of the
world, and especially thanks to that last "journey": his
agony and his death.

The Gospel passage that has just been proclaimed
helps us to understand another aspect of his human
and religious personality. We might say that among
the Apostles, he, the Successor of Peter, supremely
imitated John the "beloved disciple," who stood
under the cross with Mary at the moment of the
Redeemer's abandonment and death. The evangelist
relates that Jesus, when he saw them standing near,
entrusted the one to the other: "Woman, behold, your
son! Behold, your mother!" (Jn 19:26–27). The dying
Lord's words were particularly dear to John Paul II.

Like the Apostle and Evangelist, he too wanted to
take Mary into his home: *"et ex illa hora accepit eam dis-
cipulus in sua"* (Jn 19:27).[35] The expression *"accepit eam
in sua"* is singularly compact. It indicates John's deci-
sion to make Mary share in his own life, so as to experience that whoever opens his heart to Mary is actu-
ally accepted by her and becomes her own. The
motto that stands out in the coat of arms of the
pontificate of Pope John Paul II, *Totus tuus,* sums up
this spiritual and mystical experience well, in a life
completely oriented to Christ through Mary: *"ad
Iesum per Mariam."*

Dear brothers and sisters, this evening our
thoughts turn with emotion to the moment of the
beloved pontiff's death, but at the same time our
hearts are, as it were, impelled to look ahead. We feel
reverberating within them his repeated invitations to
advance without fear on the path of fidelity to the
Gospel, to be heralds and witnesses of Christ in the
third millennium. We cannot but recall his ceaseless
exhortations to cooperate generously in creating a
more just humanity with greater solidarity, to be
peacemakers and builders of hope. May our gaze
always remain fixed on Christ, "the same yesterday
and today and forever" (Heb 13:8), who firmly guides
his Church. We believed in his love, and it is the
encounter with him that "gives life a new horizon and
a decisive direction."[36] May the power of Jesus' Spirit

be for you all a source of peace and joy, dear brothers and sisters, as it was for Pope John Paul II. And may the Virgin Mary, Mother of the Church, help us to be, in all circumstances, as he was, tireless apostles of her divine Son and prophets of his merciful love. Amen!

Chapter VII

Pilgrims in the Footsteps of John Paul II

Pastoral Visit to Poland

May 26–28, 2006

Living One's Faith as a Relationship of Love with Christ

(Warsaw, May 26, 2006)

A hymn of gratitude to Providence

Dear brothers and sisters in Christ our Lord, "Together with you I wish to sing a hymn of praise to divine Providence, which enables me to be here as a pilgrim." Twenty-seven years ago, my beloved predecessor Pope John Paul II began his homily in Warsaw with these words. I make them my own, and I thank the Lord who has enabled me to come here today to this historic square. Here, on the eve of Pentecost, Pope John Paul II uttered the significant words of the prayer "Let your Spirit descend, and renew the face of the earth." And he added: "the face of this land." This very place witnessed the solemn funeral ceremony of the great Primate of Poland, Cardinal Stefan Wyszynski, whose twenty-fifth anniversary occurs during these days.

God united these two men not only through the same faith, hope, and love, but also through the same human vicissitudes, which linked each of them so strongly to the history of this people and of the Church that lives in their midst. At the beginning of his pontificate, Pope John Paul II wrote to Cardinal Wyszynski:

> This Polish pope would not be on the Chair of Peter today, beginning a new pontificate, full of the fear of God, but also full of trust, had it not been for your faith, which did not bend in the face of imprisonment and suffering, your heroic hope, your trusting to the end in the Mother of the Church; had it not been for Jasna Góra and this whole period of the history of the Church in our homeland, linked to your service as Bishop and Primate.[37]

How can we not thank God today for all that was accomplished in your native land and in the whole

world during the pontificate of John Paul II? Before
our eyes, changes occurred in entire political, eco-
nomic, and social systems. People in various countries regained their freedom and their sense of dignity. "Let us not forget the great works of God" (cf. Ps
78:7). I thank you, too, for your presence and for your
prayer. I thank the Cardinal Primate for the words
that he addressed to me. I greet all the bishops here
present. I am glad that the President and the authorities of [the] national and local government could be
here. I embrace with my heart all the Polish people
both at home and abroad.

Faith is an intimate relationship with Christ

"Stand firm in your faith!" We have just heard the
words of Jesus: "If you love me, you will keep my
commandments. And I will pray the Father, and he
will give you another Counselor, to be with you forever, the Spirit of truth" (Jn 14:15–17a). With these
words Jesus reveals the profound link between faith
and the profession of Divine Truth, between faith
and dedication to Jesus Christ in love, between faith
and the practice of a life inspired by the commandments. All three dimensions of faith are the fruit of
the action of the Holy Spirit. This action is manifested as an inner force that harmonizes the hearts of the

disciples with the heart of Christ and makes them capable of loving as he loved them. Hence faith is a gift, but at the same time it is a task.

"He will give you another Counselor—the Spirit of truth." Faith, as knowledge and profession of the truth about God and about man, "comes from what is heard, and what is heard comes by the preaching of Christ," as Saint Paul says (Rom 10:17). Throughout the history of the Church, the Apostles preached the word of Christ, taking care to hand it on intact to their successors, who in their turn transmitted it to subsequent generations until our own day. Many preachers of the Gospel gave their lives specifically because of their faithfulness to the truth of the word of Christ. And so solicitude for the truth gave birth to the Church's Tradition. As in past centuries, so also today there are people or groups who obscure this centuries-old Tradition, seeking to falsify the Word of Christ and to remove from the Gospel those truths that in their view are too uncomfortable for modern man. They try to give the impression that everything is relative: even the truths of faith would depend on the historical situation and on human evaluation. Yet the Church cannot silence the Spirit of Truth. The successors of the Apostles, together with the pope, are responsible for the truth of the Gospel, and all Christians are called to share in this responsibility, accepting its authoritative indications. Every

Christian is bound to confront his own convictions continually with the teachings of the Gospel and of the Church's Tradition in an effort to remain faithful to the word of Christ, even when it is demanding and, humanly speaking, hard to understand. We must not yield to the temptation of relativism or of a subjectivist and selective interpretation of Sacred Scripture. Only the whole truth can open us to adherence to Christ, dead and risen for our salvation.

Christ says: "If you love me...." Faith does not just mean accepting a certain number of abstract truths about the mysteries of God, of man, of life and death, of future realities. Faith consists of an intimate relationship with Christ, a relationship based on love of him who loved us first (cf. 1 Jn 4:11), even to the total offering of himself. "God shows his love for us in that while we were yet sinners Christ died for us" (Rom 5:8). What other response can we give to a love so great, if not that of a heart that is open and ready to love? But what does it mean to love Christ? It means trusting him even in times of trial, following him faithfully even on the *Via Crucis,* in the hope that soon the morning of the resurrection will come. Entrusting ourselves to Christ, we lose nothing, we gain everything. In his hands our life acquires its true meaning. Love for Christ expresses itself in the will to harmonize our own life with the thoughts and sentiments of his heart. This is achieved through interior union based on the grace of the Sacraments, strengthened by continuous prayer, praise, thanksgiving, and penance. We have to listen attentively to the inspirations that he evokes through his Word, through the people we meet, through the situations of daily life. To love him is to remain in dialogue with him, in order to know his will and to put it into effect promptly.

Yet living one's personal faith as a love-relationship with Christ also means being ready to renounce everything that constitutes a denial of his love. That is why Jesus said to the Apostles: "If you love me, you will keep my commandments." But what are Christ's commandments? When the Lord Jesus was teaching the crowds, he did not fail to confirm the law that the Creator had inscribed on men's hearts and had then formulated on the tablets of the Decalogue. "Think not that I have come to abolish the law and the prophets; I have come not to abolish them but to fulfill them. For truly, I say to you, till heaven and earth pass away, not an iota, not a dot, will pass from the law until all is accomplished" (Mt 5:17–18). But Jesus showed us with a new clarity the unifying center of the divine laws revealed on Sinai, namely love of God and love of neighbor: "To love [God] with all the heart, and with all the understanding, and with all the strength, and to love one's neighbor as oneself, is much more than all whole burnt offerings and sacrifices" (Mk 12:33). Indeed, in his life and in his paschal mystery, Jesus brought the entire law to completion. Uniting himself with us through the gift of the Holy Spirit, he carries with us and in us the "yoke" of the law, which thereby becomes a "light burden" (Mt 11:30). In this spirit, Jesus formulated his list of the inner qualities of those who seek to live their faith deeply: Blessed are the poor in spirit, those who weep, the meek, those who hunger and thirst for justice, the merciful, the pure in heart, the peacemakers, those who are persecuted for righteousness' sake (cf. Mt 5:3–12).

Dear brothers and sisters, faith as adherence to Christ is revealed as love that prompts us to promote the good inscribed by the Creator into the nature of every man and woman among us, into the personality of every other human being, and into everything that exists in the world. Whoever believes and loves in this way becomes a builder of the true "civilization of love," of which Christ is the center. Twenty-seven years ago, in this place, Pope John Paul II said: "Poland has become nowadays the land of a particularly responsible witness."[38] I ask you now, cultivate this rich heritage of faith transmitted to you by earlier generations, the heritage of the thought and the service of that great Pole who was Pope John Paul II. Stand firm in your faith, hand it down to your children, bear witness to the grace you have experienced so abundantly through the Holy Spirit in the course of your history. May Mary, Queen of Poland, show you the way to her Son, and may she accompany you on your journey toward a happy, peace-filled future. May your hearts never be wanting in love for Christ and his Church. Amen!

❦

"I Had to Come to the City of His Birth"

(Wadowice, Rynek Square, May 27, 2006)

Beloved brothers and sisters, I am filled with emotion in the birthplace of my great predecessor, the Servant of God John Paul II, in this town of his childhood and young adult life. Indeed, I could not leave out Wadowice as I make this pilgrimage in Poland following in his footsteps. I wished to stop precisely here, in the place where his faith began and matured, to pray together with all of you that he may soon be elevated to the glory of the altars. Johann Wolfgang von Goethe, the great German poet, said: "He who wishes to understand a poet, should visit his native land." This is also true for those who wish to understand the life and ministry of John Paul II; it is necessary to come to the city of his birth. He himself confessed that here, in Wadowice, "everything began: life, studies, the theater, and the priesthood."[39]

John Paul II, returning to his beginnings, often referred to a sign: that of the baptismal font, to which he himself gave special veneration in the Church of Wadowice. In 1979, during his first pilgrimage in Poland, he stated:

> In this baptismal font, on June 20, 1920, I was given the grace to become a son of God, together with

faith in my Redeemer, and I was welcomed into the
community of the Church. I have already solemnly
kissed this baptismal font in the year of the millennium of the Baptism of Poland, when I was Archbishop of Kraków. I kissed it again on the fiftieth
anniversary of my baptism, when I was a cardinal,
and today I kiss this baptismal font for the third
time, as I come from Rome as the Successor of Saint
Peter.[40]

It seems that in these words of John Paul II is
contained the key to understanding the consistency
of his faith, the radicalism of his Christian life, and
the desire for sanctity that he continuously manifested. Here is the profound awareness of divine grace,
the unconditional love of God for man, which by
means of water and the Holy Spirit, places the cate-
chumen among the multitude of his children who
are redeemed by the Blood of Christ. The way of an
authentically Christian life equals faithfulness to the
promises of holy Baptism. The watchword of this
pilgrimage: "Stand firm in your faith," finds in this
place its concrete dimension that can be expressed
with the exhortation: "Stand firm in the observance of
your baptismal promises." A witness of just such a
faith—of whom this place speaks in a very special
way—is the Servant of God John Paul II.

My great predecessor indicated the Basilica of
Wadowice, his home parish, as a place of particular
importance for the development of his spiritual life

and the priestly vocation that was manifesting itself within him. He once stated:

> In this church I made my first Confession and received my first Holy Communion. Here I was an altar boy. Here I gave thanks to God for the gift of the priesthood and, as Archbishop of Kraków, I celebrated the twenty-fifth anniversary of my ordination to the priesthood. God alone, the giver of every grace, knows what goodness and what manifold graces I received from this church and from this parish community. To him, the Triune God, I give glory today at the doors of this church.[41]

The Church is a sign of the communion of believers united by the presence of God who dwells in their midst. This community is the church Pope John Paul II loved. His love for the Church was born in the parish of Wadowice. In it he experienced the sacramental life, evangelization, and the formation of a mature faith. For this reason, as a priest, as a bishop, and as pope, he treated parochial communities with such great care. In the spirit of that same solicitude, during the visit *ad limina Apostolorum,* I asked the Polish bishops to do everything possible to ensure that the Polish parish would truly be an "ecclesial community" and a "family of the Church."

In conclusion, let me recall once again a characteristic of the faith and spirituality of John Paul II, which is united to this place. He himself remembered many times the deep attachment of the inhabitants of

Wadowice to the local image of Our Lady of Perpetual Help and the custom of daily prayer in front of her by the school children. This memory helps us arrive at the source of the conviction that nourished John Paul II—the conviction regarding the exceptional place that the Mother of God had in his life, a conviction that he himself, filled with devotion, expressed in the motto *Totus tuus*. Until the last moments of his earthly pilgrimage, he remained faithful to this dedication.

In the spirit of this devotion, before this image I wish to give thanks to God for the pontificate of John Paul II and, like him, I ask that Our Lady watch over the Church, which by the will of God has been entrusted to me to guide. I also ask all of you, dear brothers and sisters, to pray for me just as you prayed for your great fellow countryman. From the depths of my heart, I bless all of you present here today and all those who come to Wadowice to draw from the font of the spirit of faith of John Paul II.

❦

"With Deep Emotion I Celebrate the Eucharist in Kraków's Blonie Park"
(May 28, 2006)

"Men of Galilee, why do you stand looking up to heaven?" (Acts 1:11).

Brothers and sisters, today in Blonie Park in Kraków we hear once again this question from the Acts of the Apostles. This time it is directed to all of us: "Why do you stand looking up to heaven?" The answer to this question involves the fundamental truth about the life and destiny of every man and woman.

The question has to do with our attitude to two basic realities that shape every human life: earth and heaven. First, the earth: "Why do you stand?" Why are you here on earth? Our answer is that we are here on earth because our Maker has put us here as the crowning work of his creation. Almighty God, in his ineffable plan of love, created the universe, bringing it forth from nothing. Then, at the completion of this work, he bestowed life on men and women, creating them in his own image and likeness (cf. Gen 1:26–27). He gave them the dignity of being children of God and the gift of immortality. We know that man went astray, misused the gift of freedom and said "no" to

God, thus condemning himself to a life marked by evil, sin, suffering, and death. But we also know that God was not resigned to this situation, but entered directly into humanity's history, which then became a history of salvation. "We stand" on the earth, we are rooted in the earth and we grow from it. Here we do good in the many areas of everyday life, in the material and spiritual realms, in our relationships with other people, in our efforts to build up the human community, and in culture. Here, too, we experience the weariness of those who make their way toward a goal by long and winding paths, amid hesitations, tensions, uncertainties, in the conviction that the journey will one day come to an end. That is when the question arises: Is this all there is? Is this earth on which "we stand" our final destiny?

And so we need to turn to the second part of the biblical question: "Why do you stand looking up to heaven?" We have read that, just as the Apostles were asking the Risen Lord about the restoration of Israel's earthly kingdom, "He was lifted up and a cloud took him out of their sight," and "they looked up to heaven as he went" (cf. Acts 1:9–10). They looked up to heaven because they looked to Jesus Christ, the Crucified and Risen One, raised up on high. We do not know whether at that precise moment they realized that a magnificent, infinite horizon was opening up before their eyes: the ultimate goal of our earthly pilgrimage. Perhaps they only realized this at Pentecost, in the light of the Holy Spirit. But for us, at a distance of two thousand years, the meaning of that event is quite clear. Here on earth, we are called to look up to heaven, to turn our minds and hearts to the inexpressible mystery of God. We are called to look toward this divine reality, to which we have been directed from our creation. For there we find life's ultimate meaning.

"I wanted to breathe the air of his Poland"

Dear brothers and sisters, I am deeply moved to be able to celebrate this Eucharist today in Blonie Park in Kraków, where Pope John Paul II often celebrated Mass during his unforgettable apostolic visits to his native land. Through his liturgical celebrations he met the People of God in almost every corner of the world, but surely his celebration of Holy Mass in Blonie Park in Kraków was always something special. Here he returned in mind and heart to his roots, to the sources of his faith and his service to the Church. From here he could see Kraków and all Poland. In his first apostolic visit to Poland, on June 10, 1979, at the end of his homily in this park, he said with nostalgia: "Allow me, before leaving you, to look out once again on Kraków, this Kraków whose every stone and brick is dear to me. And to look out once again from here on Poland." During the last Mass he celebrated here, on August 18, 2002, he said in his homily: "I am grateful for the invitation to visit my Kraków and for the hospitality you have given me."[42] I wish to take up these words, to make them my own and repeat them today: I thank you with all my heart "for the invitation to visit my Kraków and for the hospitality you have given me." Kraków, the city of Karol Wojtyla and of John Paul II, is also *my Kraków!* Kraków has a special place in the hearts of countless Christians throughout the world who know that John Paul II came to the Vatican Hill from this city, from Wawel Hill, "from a far country," which thus became a country dear to all.

At the beginning of the second year of my pontificate, I have felt a deep need to visit Poland and Kraków as a pilgrim in the footsteps of my predecessor. I wanted to breathe the air of his homeland. I wanted to see the land where he was born, where he grew up and undertook his tireless service to Christ and the universal Church. I wanted especially to meet the living men and women of his country, to experience your faith, which gave him life and strength, and to know that you continue firm in that faith. Here I wish to ask God to preserve that legacy of faith, hope, and charity that John Paul II gave to the world, and to you in particular.

"Remain firm in the faith"

I cordially greet all those gathered in Blonie Park, for as far as my eyes can see and even farther. I wish I could meet each of you personally. I embrace all those who are taking part in our Eucharist by radio and television. I greet all of Poland! I greet the children and young people, individuals and families, the sick and those suffering in body or spirit, who are deprived of the joy of life. I greet all those whose daily labors are helping this country to grow in prosperity. I greet the Polish people living abroad, everywhere in the world. I thank Cardinal Stanislaw Dziwisz, the Metropolitan Archbishop of Kraków, for his warm words of welcome. I greet Cardinal Franciszek Macharski and all the cardinals, bishops, priests, and consecrated men and women, as well as the other guests who have come from many lands, particularly the neighboring countries. My greetings go to the President of the Republic and to the Prime Minister, and to the representatives of the national, territorial, and local authorities.

Dear brothers and sisters, I have taken as the motto of my pilgrimage to Poland in the footsteps of John Paul II the words: "Stand firm in your faith!" This appeal is directed to us all as members of the community of Christ's disciples, to each and every one of us. Faith is a deeply personal and human act, an act that has two aspects. To believe means first to accept as true what our mind cannot fully comprehend. We have to accept what God reveals to us about himself, about ourselves, about everything around us, including the things that are invisible, inexpressible, and beyond our imagination. This act of accepting revealed truth broadens the horizon of our knowledge and draws us to the mystery in which our lives are immersed. Letting our reason be limited in this way is not something easy to do. Here we see the second aspect of faith: it is trust in a person, no ordinary person, but Jesus Christ himself. What we believe is important, but even more important is the One in whom we believe.

Saint Paul speaks of this in the passage from the Letter to the Ephesians that we have heard today. God has given us a spirit of wisdom and

> enlightened the eyes of our hearts, that we may know what is the hope to which he has called us, the riches of his glorious inheritance in the saints, and the immeasurable greatness of his power in us who believe, according to the working of his great power in Christ. (cf. Eph 1:17–20)

Believing means surrendering ourselves to God and entrusting our destiny to him. Believing means entering into a personal relationship with our Creator and Redeemer in the power of the Holy Spirit, and making this relationship the basis of our whole life.

Today we heard the words of Jesus: "You shall receive power when the Holy Spirit has come upon you; and you shall be my witnesses in Jerusalem and in all Judea and Samaria, and to the end of the earth" (Acts 1:8). Centuries ago these words reached Poland. They challenged and continue to challenge all those who say they belong to Christ, who consider his to be the greatest cause. We need to be witnesses of Jesus, who lives in the Church and in human hearts. He has given us a mission. On the day he ascended to heaven, he said to his Apostles:

> "Go into all the world and preach the Gospel to the whole creation...." And they went forth and preached everywhere, while the Lord worked with them and confirmed the message by the signs that attended it. (Mk 16:15, 20)

Dear brothers and sisters! When Karol Wojtyla was elected to the See of Peter in order to serve the universal Church, your land became a place of special witness to faith in Jesus Christ. You were called to give this witness before the whole world. This vocation of yours is always needed, and it is perhaps even more urgent than ever, now that the Servant of God has passed from this life. Do not deprive the world of this witness!

Before I return to Rome to continue my ministry, I appeal to all of you in the words spoken here by Pope John Paul II in 1979:

You must be strong, dear brothers and sisters. You
must be strong with the strength that comes from
faith. You must be strong with the strength of faith.
You must be faithful. Today, more than in any other
age, you need this strength. You must be strong with
the strength of hope, the hope that brings perfect
joy in life and that prevents us from ever grieving
the Holy Spirit! You must be strong with love, the
love that is stronger than death.... You must be
strong with the strength of faith, hope, and charity,
a charity that is conscious, mature, and responsible,
and which can help us at this moment of our history to carry on the great dialogue with man and the
world, a dialogue rooted in dialogue with God himself, with the Father, through the Son, in the Holy
Spirit, the dialogue of salvation.[43]

I, too, Benedict XVI, the successor of Pope John
Paul II, am asking you to look up from earth to heav-
en, to lift your eyes to the One to whom succeeding
generations have looked for two thousand years, and in
whom they have discovered life's ultimate meaning.
Strengthened by faith in God, devote yourselves fer-
vently to consolidating his kingdom on earth, a kingdom of goodness, justice, solidarity, and mercy. I ask
you to bear courageous witness to the Gospel before
today's world, bringing hope to the poor, the suffering,
the lost and abandoned, the desperate, and those
yearning for freedom, truth, and peace. By doing good
to your neighbor and showing your concern for the
common good, you bear witness that God is love.

I ask you, finally, to share with the other peoples of Europe and the world the treasure of your faith, not least as a way of honoring the memory of your countryman, who, as the Successor of Saint Peter, did this with extraordinary power and effectiveness. And remember me in your prayers and sacrifices, even as you remembered my great predecessor, so that I can carry out the mission Christ has given me. I ask you to stand firm in your faith! Stand firm in your hope! Stand firm in your love! Amen!

John Paul II:
Gift to the Church and the World

We Commemorate My Great Predecessor's Election to the See of Peter

October 16, 2006

Dear brothers and sisters, today, October 16, the day on which we commemorate the election of Karol Wojtyla to the See of Peter, I wish to unite myself spiritually with you in prayerful thanks for the pontificate of my great predecessor. So please accept my cordial greeting.

I want to return with you in memory to the unforgettable day of his election to the See of Peter. I still hear the echo of his words—humble, wise, and full of devotion—when he replied to the question of whether he accepted the choice made by the cardinals: "In the obedience of faith before Christ my Lord, trusting in the Mother of Christ and of the Church, and aware of the great difficulties—I accept!" I can see him before me, strong and serene, on the balcony of Saint Peter's Basilica, when for the first time he gave the blessing *Urbi et Orbi,* entrusting himself to the protection of the Virgin Mary and to the love of those all over the world for whom he had to care as pastor and guide. I have never forgotten his prophetic summons: "Be not afraid! Open the doors to Christ!" I thank God that, with these images in my heart, I was able to spend more than two decades at his side, enjoying his benevolence and friendship, and that today I can continue his work beneath his protective gaze from the Father's house. I thank God for his life spent in love for Christ and for others, which has enriched the lives of all humanity through the grace of the Holy Spirit, in an attitude of brotherhood and peace. Finally, I thank God for the witness of his suffering united with the tribulation of Christ, even to death—a witness that gives us the strength to live and reinforces our hope in eternal life.

How dear to John Paul II was the Church in Poland! How many times he gave expression to this sentiment! He loved it like a mother who had given him life in the faith and had raised him in love for Christ and for his brethren. But he also loved it as a community always united around its pastors, exposed in the past to suffering through various persecutions, but always faithful to the evangelical values. How he prayed, and how he struggled so that Poland might win its freedom back! And when this happened, he did not slacken his efforts so that his fellow country-men might keep their faith and learn to live in the freedom of the children of God, and not as the chil-dren of this world.

Aware of this heritage that he has left to the Church in Poland, I have come among you this year with the Pauline exhortation: "Remain strong in the faith." On this occasion, I would like once again to thank you for the witness of living faith that you gave in those times imbued with the Spirit, and that brought joy to my heart. I pray that God may pre-serve the faith for the future generations of this noble land. I thank you in a special way for all the signs of loving union with the pope that you have shown to your great countryman. I entrust to your spiritual support my service to the Church and to the world.

Finally, on this day I greet with joy all the people of Poland. May the memory of John Paul II and the study of his work and his teaching bring you closer to Christ. May these be the nucleus of unity in a shared struggle for the future of the Church and of the nation. I extend my heartfelt blessing to all, in the name of the Father, and of the Son, and of the Holy Spirit.

Sources

CHAPTER I

John Paul II: Unity of Mission and Person. Written for the twentieth year of John Paul's pontificate and published for the first time under the title *Giovanni Paolo II: Venti anni di pontificato* (*John Paul II: Twenty Years of His Pontificate*). Cinisello Balsamo (Milan): San Paolo, 1998, pp. 7–31.

CHAPTER II

The Faith Is Humanity's Refuge: The Fourteen Encyclicals of John Paul II was published by *Communio*, Italian edition, nn. 190–191, July–October 2003, pp. 8–16.

CHAPTER III

Roman Triptych: Meditations. Presentation by Cardinal Joseph Ratzinger. March 6, 2003. http://www.vatican.va/holy_

father/john_paul_ii/books/documents/hf_jp-ii_books_
20030306_presentation-trittico-romano_en.html.

Chapter IV

"Our Beloved Pope Now Stands at the Window of the Father's
House." Homily of His Eminence Cardinal Joseph
Ratzinger at the funeral Mass of the Roman Pontiff John
Paul II. Saint Peter's Square, April 8, 2005. http://www.vat-
ican.va/gpII/documents/homily-card-ratzinger_
20050408_en.html.

Chapter V

"Let Yourselves be Surprised by Christ!" Apostolic Journey to
Cologne on the Occasion of the Twentieth World Youth
Day. Address of His Holiness Pope Benedict XVI at the
celebration welcoming the young people. Cologne, August
18, 2005. http://www.vatican.va/holy_father/benedict_xvi
/speeches/2005/august/documents/hf_ben-xvi_spe_
20050818_youth-celebration_en.html.

Chapter VI

The Angelus message was delivered by Pope Benedict XVI in
Saint Peter's Square, on April 2, 2006. http://www.vati-
can.va/holy_father/benedict_xvi/angelus/2006/docu-
ments/hf_ben-xvi_ang_20060402_en.html.

The Holy Rosary was prayed on April 2, 2006, with reflections
by Pope Benedict XVI. http://www.vatican.va/holy_father
/benedict_xvi/speeches/2006/april/documents/hf_ben-
xvi_spe_20060402_rosary_en.html.

The homily was delivered by Pope Benedict XVI in the Papal Chapel on April 3, 2006. http://www.vatican.va/holy_father /benedict_xvi/homilies/2006/documents/hf_ben- xvi_hom_20060403_anniv-death-jp-ii_en.html.

Chapter VII

"Pilgrims in the Footsteps of John Paul II": Pastoral Visit to Poland. Pastoral Visit of His Holiness Pope Benedict XVI to Poland.

Homily by the Holy Father. Mass in Pilsudzki Square, Warsaw, May 26, 2006. http://www.vatican.va/holy_father/bene- dict_xvi/homilies/2006/documents/hf_ben-xvi_hom_ 20060526_varsavia_en.html.

Greeting of the Holy Father, Wadowice, Rynek Square, May 27, 2006. http://www.vatican.va/holy_father/benedict_xvi /speeches/2006/may/documents/hf_ben-xvi_ spe_20060527_wadowice_en.html.

Homily by the Holy Father at the Mass in Kraków-Blonie, May 28, 2006. http://www.vatican.va/holy_father/benedict_xvi /homilies/2006/documents/hf_ben-xvi_hom_ 20060528_krakow_en.html.

Conclusion

"We Commemorate My Great Predecessor's Election to the See of Peter" (October 16, 2006). The Italian text can be found on the site dedicated to the cause of the beatification and canonization of John Paul II: http://www.vicariatusurbis. org/Beatificazione.html.

Notes

1. Letter of John Paul II to Cardinal Joseph Ratzinger on the fiftieth anniversary of his ordination. From the Vatican, June 20, 2002, © Libreria Editrice Vaticana. http://www.vatican.va/holy_father_john_paul_ii/letters/2001/documents/hf_jpii_let_20010628_ ratzinger-50-priesthood_en.html.

2. "Pope" in Italian. — Ed.

3. Pope John Paul II. — Ed.

4. Used here and elsewhere in the sense of Aristotelian and Thomistic philosophy. — Trans.

5. *Gaudium et Spes.* — Ed.

6. *Redemptoris Mater.* — Ed.

7. World Youth Day, 1997. — Ed.

8. 1997. — Ed.

9. The encyclical *Fides et Ratio* was published on October 15, 1998.

10. *Orientale Lumen,* 3.

11. *Redemptor Hominis,* 22.

12. *Ecclesia de Eucharistia,* 2003. — Ed.

13. *Redemptor Hominis,* 18.

14. Ibid., 14.

15. Ibid., 13.

16. Ibid., 14.

17. Ibid., 8.

18. *Dominum et Vivificantem,* 31.

19. Ibid., 36.

20. Ibid., 45.

21. Used here in the sense of the political philosophy underlying, for example, the American and French revolutions in the eighteenth century, and *not* in its twentieth-century meaning. — Trans.

22. *Veritatis Splendor,* 40.

23. "Dare to know!"

24. The Redeemer of man. — Ed.

25. From the Latin, *clavis,* meaning "key." — Ed.

26. *Memory and Identity,* p. 55.

27. Ibid., p. 167.

28. The original Greek for this phrase. — Ed.

29. "To the city and to the world."

30. *Saint Peter Chrysologus,* Serm., 160, 2.

31. *Homily at the Mass of Inauguration,* April 24, 2005.

32. *Inauguration Homily, L'Osservatore Romano* English edition, November 2, 1978, p. 12.

33. *Salvifici Doloris,* 30.

34. *Gift and Mystery,* cf. pp. 101–114.

35. "…and from that hour the disciple took her into his own home."

36. Cf. *Deus Caritas Est*, 1.

37. *Letter of Pope John Paul II to the Polish People*, October 23, 1978.

38. Warsaw, June 2, 1979.

39. Wadowice, June 16, 1999.

40. Wadowice, June 7, 1979.

41. Wadowice, June 16, 1999.

42. No. 2.

43. *Homily*, June 10, 1979, 4.

Pauline
BOOKS & MEDIA

The Daughters of St. Paul operate book and media centers at the following addresses. Visit, call or write the one nearest you today, or find us on the World Wide Web, www.pauline.org

CALIFORNIA

3908 Sepulveda Blvd, Culver City, CA 90230	310-397-8676
2460 Broadway Street, Redwood City, CA 94063	650-369-4230
5945 Balboa Avenue, San Diego, CA 92111	858-565-9181

FLORIDA

145 S.W. 107th Avenue, Miami, FL 33174	305-559-6715

HAWAII

1143 Bishop Street, Honolulu, HI 96813	808-521-2731
Neighbor Islands call:	866-521-2731

ILLINOIS

172 North Michigan Avenue, Chicago, IL 60601	312-346-4228

LOUISIANA

4403 Veterans Memorial Blvd, Metairie, LA 70006	504-887-7631

MASSACHUSETTS

885 Providence Hwy, Dedham, MA 02026	781-326-5385

MISSOURI

9804 Watson Road, St. Louis, MO 63126	314-965-3512

NEW JERSEY

561 U.S. Route 1, Wick Plaza, Edison, NJ 08817	732-572-1200

NEW YORK

150 East 52nd Street, New York, NY 10022	212-754-1110

PENNSYLVANIA

9171-A Roosevelt Blvd, Philadelphia, PA 19114	215-676-9494

SOUTH CAROLINA

243 King Street, Charleston, SC 29401	843-577-0175

TENNESSEE

4811 Poplar Avenue, Memphis, TN 38117	901-761-2987

TEXAS

114 Main Plaza, San Antonio, TX 78205	210-224-8101

VIRGINIA

1025 King Street, Alexandria, VA 22314	703-549-3806

CANADA

3022 Dufferin Street, Toronto, ON M6B 3T5	416-781-9131

¡También somos su fuente para libros,
videos y música en español!